SPINNING
FOR TROUT

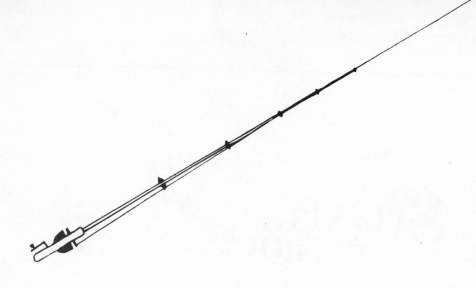

Other books by Bob Gooch

THE WEEDY WORLD OF THE PICKERELS
SQUIRRELS AND SQUIRREL HUNTING
BASS FISHING
IN SEARCH OF THE WILD TURKEY
COVEYS AND SINGLES
LAND YOU CAN HUNT

SPINNING FOR TROUT

How to Catch Rainbows, Browns, Brookies, and Others by This Effective, Easy-to-Learn Method

BOB GOOCH

Drawings by Pat Gooch

CHARLES SCRIBNER'S SONS · NEW YORK

First Charles Scribner's Sons paperback edition 1984

Library of Congress Cataloging in Publication Data

Gooch, Bob, 1919–
  Spinning for trout.
  Includes index.
  1. Trout fishing.   2.   Spin-fishing.   I.   Title.
SH687.G64   799.1'755   81–225
ISBN 0-684-18076-6   AACR2

1 3 5 7 9 11 13 15 17 19   F/P   20 18 16 14 12 10 8 6 4 2

Printed in the United States of America

To
Pam and Pat

Acknowledgments

Help for a book on fishing comes from many sources and many people—biologists, fellow anglers, fellow scribes, and others. It comes informally, unselfishly, and through the seasons both good and bad. Sorting out the accumulated knowledge bit by bit and crediting the proper people would be an impossible task. But unlike most anglers, I am presented with a golden opportunity— a chance to thank those who over the years have shared their knowledge with me. I do so emphatically.

Some of those fine anglers I have not seen for years and may never see again. But we share many fond memories.

Harold Tate, a former president of the Virginia Chapter of Trout Unlimited and an avid angler, gave me the idea for this book. A dedicated fly fisherman, he recognized the need for a book on spinning for trout—possibly because he has a young son just learning to fish.

One of life's greatest disappointments has been my inability to make serious anglers out of my wife, Ginny, and our two daughters, Pam and Pat. Still, they are a constant source of encouragement. We have shared many outdoor experiences, and their enthusiasm for my modest angling achievements is always warming.

Chet Fish, my editor at Scribners, has been wading through my assorted literary efforts since his early days at *Outdoor Life* magazine. I am sure his unrelenting scrutiny of my work has kept me out of trouble, and I am grateful.

Finally, there are the fishery-management people across this land—the biologists, the hatchery workers, the wardens, and others whose dedicated efforts have maintained our trout populations at satisfactory levels. Without them there would be little trout fishing in America today, and I would not have been inspired to write a book about it.

Bob Gooch
Troy, Virginia

Contents

Preface

Two ideas played tag in my mind as I wrote the final pages of this book.

I learned anew, as I had in writing previous books, that regardless of how much a fishing writer knows about his subject, he is a better angler for having written about it—if for no other reason than that it makes him organize his thoughts. He must take a more penetrating look at techniques he has used successfully for years. He must be able to support them, to look at them through the objective eyes of the reader. It is truly a soul-searching task.

The other idea was provoked by the pile of unused notes on my desk, good information that a book of this length simply cannot accommodate. Spinning for trout is a broad and varied subject, and a single book cannot possibly delve into all of its many facets. It is a beginning, however, and maybe some other writer will take the subject from here.

For my part, I have concentrated on the trouts that over 90 percent of anglers fish for—the brook, brown, and rainbow, and to a lesser extent the cutthroat.

It's surprising that top-notch anglers who are fly fishermen are often also accomplished spinning anglers—except when it comes to trout. Many of these people seem to feel it an insult to the dignity of a trout to take it on anything but a flyrod. Some even support the idea that only dry flies should be used to take this noble fish.

I share with them this love of the flyrod, and I enjoy nothing more than taking wary browns or native brookies on dainty dry flies. But trout fishing does not end there.

The great majority of average and beginning trout fishermen fish with spinning tackle. These fishermen are also anglers, and in the truest sense. They too buy fishing licenses, obey the laws, support conservation programs, and make their contributions to society.

They too enjoy trout fishing, and this book is for them.

The book is written in such a way that you can either read it straight through or pick out the parts that particularly interest you and read those first. Because you may be dipping into the text at different spots according to which type of trout you are pursuing or which type of water you are fishing, I have repeated certain bits of essential information so that you will not miss them, regardless of where you start reading.

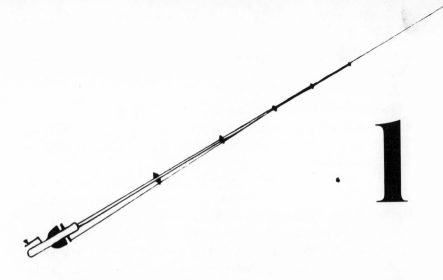

Why Spinning?

Why a book on spinning for trout? It's a fair question.

Outdoor scribes have been writing about trout for generations. Izaak Walton's classic *The Compleat Angler*, published more than three hundred years ago, speaks of fly fishing for trout and "twelve flies for every month." Since that distant year, countless books have been devoted to the trout. Many have joined *The Compleat Angler* as angling classics, and the vast majority—like that early one—have centered on fly fishing.

While spinning for trout has received the attention of angling editors, newspaper columnists, magazine writers, and movie producers, book authors have generally directed their trout efforts toward the fine art of fly fishing.

I certainly have nothing against fly fishing. In fact, I love the sport. In my early years, I took many trout on a battered old split-bamboo flyrod, and in my eternal search for the perfect one I have accumulated more flyrods than I can count on the fingers of my two hands.

But the spinning angler deserves attention also.

Today, the casual angler, the beginner, the eager young fisherman, almost invariably turn to spinning tackle for trout fishing. Though fly fishing is within the capability of most anglers, spinning is easier to master.

While fly fishing is our oldest form of angling, spinning is our youngest. When you consider that spinning first hit America in the late 1940s, it is a mere infant by comparison.

My own introduction to spinning was far from sensational. One of my favorite fishing partners during the late 1940s was a TWA pilot who made frequent flights to Europe. An eager angler, he was ever alert for fishing-tackle bargains. So during a layover in Paris, he picked up a light spinning rod and an open-face reel. Spinning was popular in Europe long before it was introduced to America.

"Let me show you something," Herb said when he knocked on my door.

We took the little rod and reel out to the grassy court of the apartment complex we then lived in and gave spinning a try. We found the tackle easy to handle and soon got the knack of it. But neither of us was impressed. Possibly we were handicapped by the braided silk line, the only kind available for spinning tackle then.

I forgot about spinning and went back to my conventional fly-fishing and baitcasting tackle.

Within a few years, however, I was caught up in the spinning craze as it swept across the fishing waters of the United States and Canada. American tackle manufacturers got into the act and introduced the now-popular monofilament line to the fishing world.

I bought a tough little Wright and McGill fiberglass rod for $6.05, an Airex Bache Brown open-face spinning reel for $13.50, a six-pound-test line, and half a dozen small lures. Since that long-ago day, both my fly-fishing and baitcasting tackle have seen less use.

Once spinning tackle caught on, it proved so effective that many conservative anglers even expressed concern for the fish populations. "Spinning tackle will clean out our waters," they wailed.

The ease with which it can be mastered has no doubt attracted

While fishing with ultralight spinning tackle, the author took this fine rainbow trout from the Williams River in West Virginia.
Photo by Pat Gooch

Johnny Gooch, the author's nephew, dons waders before entering the Hughes River in Virginia for opening day. Because spinning is easy to learn, it is a good way to introduce a young angler to trout fishing.

Spinning tackle is ideal for opening day, when crowded conditions on most streams leave little room for the back-cast of the fly fisherman.

many trout fishermen to spinning tackle. Even the beginner, with a bit of help from an experienced angler, can be making acceptable casts soon after his introduction to the tackle.

Crowded conditions on put-and-take trout waters have also contributed to the popularity of spinning tackle. The fly fisherman needs space for effective casting. His back-cast is a hazard to other anglers, and frustration is bound to be one result of a crowded opening day. To accommodate the fly fisherman, many states have even designated some streams for fly fishing only. Many veteran fly fishermen have turned to spinning for crowded put-and-take streams, reserving their fly tackle for later in the season when the crowds thin out.

But spinning is much more than a tool for the beginner or the inexperienced, or a substitute for fly fishing under adverse conditions. It is a highly versatile form of angling that will take trout under conditions that would prove insurmountable to the flyrod

Spinning is not only a good way to introduce a young angler to trout fishing but is also a highly versatile system that will take trout under a variety of conditions. This three-pound rainbow trout was caught in Virginia's Douthat Lake while the author was working a streamer deep on light spinning tackle.

man. Spoons, for example, will take trout when nothing else will, but spoons are just about impossible on the flyrod.

Before the advent of spinning tackle, tiny lures such as plugs, spoons, and the various spinner–fly combination lures were popular among some fly fishermen, but they never handled well on fly tackle. In comparison to the average wet or dry fly, such lures were heavy, wind-resistant, and generally cumbersome to cast.

Spinning tackle solved this problem for the trout fisherman. The flexible spinning outfit seemed made to order for the tiny lures. They are rarely fished by fly fishermen anymore. When their use is appropriate, the average trout fisherman uses them on spinning tackle.

Furthermore, the various natural baits—minnows, worms of all kinds, crickets, grubs, and even salmon eggs—handle better on spinning tackle than they do on fly tackle. Delivering a natural bait to a tight spot in a stream was always a difficult feat on the flyrod because bait does not lend itself well to the fly cast. The spinning angler, on the other hand, can deliver a soft cast, one that will not

Thin monofilament spinning line is an asset when fishing fast water. Johnny Gooch (foreground) fishes a fast stretch of Virginia's South River.

Thin monofilament spinning line is also an asset when fishing deep water.

tear the bait loose. And he can do so with fair accuracy. He can also cast his bait farther than can the fly fisherman.

Most trout fishermen also find spinning tackle more practical in fast water, where—by contrast—a heavy fly line can be cumbersome in the powerful current. The thin monofilament spinning line is easy to control, less resistant to the current.

Deep water is also less of a problem when the angler is fishing with spinning tackle. Small sinkers and weighted lures, awkward to handle on a flyrod, are no problem on spinning tackle.

Even the most dedicated fly fisherman will find good use for spinning tackle on trout waters today.

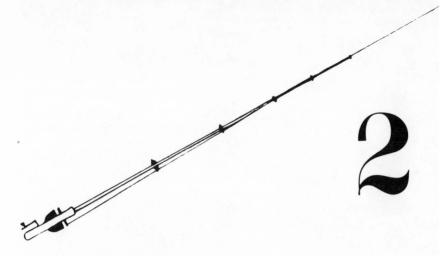

Spinning Tackle

Having logged many pleasant hours, days, and seasons flyfishing for trout, I did not rush out and buy a spinning outfit when the craze first hit American waters. I was content with what I had. Eventually, though, I yielded. I could see definite possibilities for such tackle on some of my favorite trout waters.

My first spinning tackle, described in Chapter 1, was modest. Except for the line, which was too heavy, I still own all that tackle. But I seldom use it anymore.

I caught trout on it, too—brilliantly marked native brook trout; hatchery-reared brooks, browns, and rainbows; and even a few cut-throats on a family camping trip in the west. With that tackle, I learned about spinning and how to adapt it to trout fishing.

I also learned early that some modifications in my tackle would improve my fishing skills and my chances for success. For example,

Basic spinning tackle: an open-face spinning reel, monofilament line, light rod, and a tackle bag. Such gear is easy to pack on trips into the back-country.

my first line was too heavy for precision casting, and besides, I didn't need that much line strength on the flexible-glass rod.

I have since acquired half a dozen spinning rods and more spinning reels than I need. I have experimented with all kinds of lines.

In recent years, I have settled on ultralight spinning tackle for much of my trout fishing. My little five-foot, two-ounce Fenwick rod is built for lures of one-sixteenth to one-fourth ounce and lines testing one to four pounds. Most of the time I fish a two-pound-test line on a tiny Orvis reel. This outfit is adequate for most of the fish I encounter in the trout streams of my native Virginia and elsewhere in America and Canada.

I own another ultralight spinning reel, however, that is loaded with four-pound-test line. I use it on those rare occasions when I think a heavier line is prudent. A third reel is spooled with thread-like one-pound-test monofilament for fishing the tiny headwaters for native brookies that rarely are longer than eight or nine inches.

"You can accomplish the same thing," an angling friend reminded me, "by carrying different lines on extra spools for one reel." But I like to collect ultralight spinning reels.

This light tackle is easy to pack and a delight to fish with. And the thin line improves my chances considerably.

Such an outfit will handle much of the trout fishing available in North America today, most of which is for stocked brooks, browns, and rainbows that rarely weigh more than a pound. I can handle larger trout, however, if I go to my light tackle with the four-pound-test line. On it I have taken a four-pound rainbow in Virginia's Douthat Lake, a big cutthroat that surprised me on a small Wyoming stream, and even a four-pound smallmouth bass that had invaded a favorite brown-trout stream.

The Rod

The typical spinning rod is used with an open-face reel. Most such rods have a pair of handles, with the reel seated at a fixed spot below and between the two. On a spinning rod with a single handle, the reel can be shifted forward or backward for better balance.

In the angling position, the reel is below your casting hand. If you're right-handed, you cast with your right hand and crank the reel handle with your left. The reverse is true for the left-handed caster.

My little five-foot, two-ounce Fenwick spinning rod is one of the daintiest. It is a good choice for brookies, small cutthroats, and put-and-take brooks, browns, and rainbows that average eight to ten inches. It's also fine for goldens, creek Dolly Vardens, the Yellowstone trout, and trout such as the Piute and Gila.

At the other extreme is the big spinning rod built for casting hefty lures and bait into the ocean surf. I own one of those, a sturdy, hollow-glass, nine-foot, ten-ounce Shakespeare rod capable of handling just about any trout that swims. Actually, it is of limited value to the trout angler except possibly for lunker steelheads (sea-going rainbows), big Kamloops trout, lakers, big arctic char, and big lake cutthroats. Most of these trout, though, are taken on much lighter tackle.

The spinning rod used for lake trout should be sturdy but also flexible enough for you to detect the gentle strike of the fish. That rod should also have the capacity to deliver a long cast.

The conventional steelhead rod may go six to eight ounces.

"I like a light rod, a step up from ultralight for steelhead," says David Richey, a noted Michigan outdoor writer and steelhead angler.

The great variety of spinning rods includes light ones and heavy ones, short ones and long ones, flexible ones for worms and other natural baits, and rods with sturdy butt sections. A six- to eight-foot, medium-action rod with a reasonably sturdy butt section, however, will handle just about any trout fishing the average angler will encounter, including most steelheads, sea-run brooks and browns, spring lakers in the shallows, arctic chars, and cutthroats from larger waters. Such a rod will weigh from five to seven ounces.

I lean toward the lightest rod that will do the job. With it, I can handle a greater variety of lures, cast better, and derive more enjoyment from the exciting battle with a trout. There is no reason to skimp, however, thereby risking the loss of a good fish. Experience and judgment are the best guides. The rod used to fish swollen spring waters, for example, should be heavier than that employed later in the season when there is less current to buck.

The Reel

Ultralight reels, watch-size little wonders that are a joy to fish with, are the most prized ones in my tackle box, and they serve yeoman's duty. They are a bit fragile and require care in handling. They should be lubricated frequently when subjected to heavy use. I own three, an Orvis, a Mitchell, and a Shakespeare, each loaded with line of a different strength so I can switch from one line to another without changing spools. Each ultralight weighs six to seven ounces.

The other extreme in spinning reels is the big saltwater surf-fishing reel that goes with the nine-foot surf rod. It too is a Mitchell, a big sturdy eighteen-ouncer. I use it with the surf rod only.

My ultralight reels see occasional use on one of my medium-weight spinning rods if the situation demands it or if I happen to break my ultralight rod and need a two- or four-pound-test line for a given situation. This would be an emergency measure. Best results are achieved when the spinning rod, reel, and line are in balance with one another.

Reels for the six- to eight-foot medium-action rods are larger than the ultralights but much smaller than the surf reel. These mid-weights are usually classified as nine- to twelve-ounce reels. Such reels can be spooled with lines ranging from four- to twelve-pound test, but there is seldom any reason to go above a six- to eight-pound-test line on medium-weight spinning tackle. The lighter line casts better, permits a wider choice of lures, and is less conspicuous to the trout.

Spinning reels, the ultralight models in particular, are delicate instruments and more susceptible to breakdown than most reels. A spare is good insurance. In a pinch, an ultralight reel will serve on a medium-weight spinning rod or a sizable reel can be used on an ultralight rod.

All spinning reels require reasonable care and maintenance. They should be lubricated frequently. Bails, particularly, seem to get out of whack quickly. They should be given frequent attention. Drags are delicate. They should be set just below the breaking strength of the line.

The open-face spinning reel is the very heart of spinning, and you should not skimp on quality. All of the leading tackle companies turn out good ones. Daiwa, Garcia, Orvis, Shakespeare, and South Bend are represented in my tackle box. They all get heavy use and serve me well. And when other than a routine repair is indicated, they go home to the manufacturer for expert attention.

Spinning tackle is not foolproof. True, there is no problem of a backlash, but those "line sloughs" on an open-face reel can be frustrating. They seem to happen just when the fishing is best. This problem is usually the result of a badly twisted line caused by revolving lures. The best way to avoid a line slough is to check the line periodically for signs of twist. You can eliminate the twist by removing the lure and letting the line run out in a stretch of fast water. Or when you're on a lake or pond, run the bare line out behind a fast-moving boat.

Most of my medium-weight reels are loaded with six-pound-test line. It casts well and has sufficient strength for most of the fish I

take on this tackle. For larger trout, however, I don't hesitate to go
to ten-, twelve-, fifteen-, or even twenty-pound-test line. The heavier line does deprive me of casting distance. The six-pound-test line
is a good choice for most trout fishing. I personally prefer four-
pound test, and I often use two-pound test. It is a rare situation that
demands a line testing more than eight pounds.

"Took it on a six-pound-test line," I announced happily when
some companions in a Quebec fishing camp recently asked me what
I had landed a fine ten-pound lake trout on.

The spinning reel has a fixed spool. Unlike the baitcasting reel,
the reel does not revolve when a cast is made. The thin line simply
peels off of the stationary spool. Absence of a backlash risk is a
major reason spinning can be mastered so quickly by the novice.
When you retrieve, the line is guided back onto the reel by the bail.

The fixed-spool principle is a simple but highly effective method
of handling a fishing line. To say that it revolutionized trout fishing
around the world is an understatement.

The big saltwater spinning reel employs the same principle. It is
just sturdier and has the capacity for many yards of heavy monofilament line. It's my choice for big-water steelheads, lakers, arctic
chars, and outsized lake cutthroats. Steelheads are simply rainbows that migrate between the streams and ocean.

The Line

Modern monofilament spinning line is a thing of joy. Tough and
almost invisible in the water, it is a tremendous angling asset. I use
the lightest line that is practical. In fact, I have often been guilty of
using too light a line and paid for my mistake by losing good trout.
Still, I am sure my thin line has produced strikes when the trout
would have shied off from heavier line. Such things have a way of
balancing out.

An early problem with monofilament was its tendency to become
stiff and wiry during cold weather. Today's softer line does not
present this problem. Line twist, though, is still a problem. It causes
kinks and line sloughs that make the line just about impossible to
fish with. Small ball-bearing swivels between line and lure help
reduce line twist, but many anglers don't like to use swivels. I'm

among them. I prefer tying the line directly to the lure. Small spinning lures are highly sensitive, and many anglers believe the swivel hampers the delicate action.

In the preceding section on reels, I described how to remove line twist.

Flat or ribbon-type monofilament line is more likely to twist than round line.

The need for balance in your spinning outfit is particularly true of the line. Usually, the lighter line permits you to get greater distance and more accuracy in your casts. It is just about impossible to attain good distance and accuracy when the line is too heavy for the rod, reel, and lure.

If you hook an unusually heavy fish and you fear the combined pressure of fish and current will be too much for your thin line, you can follow the fish. Stream fish will usually head downstream. On a lake or pond, you can follow the trout in your boat and take pressure off your light tackle.

Ultralight line should be used only on ultralight tackle. A two- to four-pound-test line should not be used on a heavy rod. The stiffer rod may pop the line when you set the hook in a good trout. A heavy lure will quickly wear out a thin line, and it is impossible to cast a light lure effectively on a heavy line.

In addition to the conventional misty-blue lines, there are a variety of colored ones on the market. They are easy for the angler to see and follow in the water, but nearly invisible to the trout. Your ability to spot a line in the water can be helpful. On a stream you can follow the path of your lure. And if you like to watch the movement of your line for a strike, the color is a definite advantage.

You should own a variety of lines for the varied water and fishing conditions you may encounter. One way is to buy extra reel spools and load each with a different line. Switching spools can be done quickly on the stream or lake. If you own spare reels, you can load them with different types of line. A spare reel can save a fishing trip.

Terminal Tackle

I have just about eliminated terminal tackle from my fishing, but some anglers like to use tiny swivels to prevent line twist. My only advice is to buy the best. Swivels that do not work are a hindrance. Ball-bearing swivels are a good choice.

Some anglers like tiny snaps to facilitate changing lures. Usually, snaps come in combination with swivels. Snaps are handy, but I prefer to break the lure off and tie the next one directly to the line. The terminal end of a line gets heavy wear anyway. It tends to fray badly and should be cut off frequently and retied.

A number of proven knots can be used to tie lures to lines. Try the Palomar knot, the basic uni-knot, or the simple or improved clinch knot. Where the fish run small and there is little risk of their breaking off, I sometimes tie a simple bowline in the end of my line. Then I run its loop through the eye of the lure, over the lure, and back toward the eye. Finally, I pull the loop snug against the eye. And I can remove the lure without breaking the line by simply reversing the procedure.

For big lake trout and other trout that have teeth on the tongue that may cut the line, some anglers use a leader. This is usually a "shock" leader of heavier monofilament a few inches long, but wire is sometimes used.

Miscellaneous Equipment

I'll discuss lures in detail in later chapters, but here let's talk about other odds and ends of spinning tackle you need in your pursuit of the trout.

For carrying the great variety of tackle the average angler packs, you need a tackle box or a bag.

The boat fisherman can fill this requirement with a light box designed for spinning tackle. These boxes are smaller than the typical bass-fishing tackle box. Rarely does the trout fisherman use the wide variety of lures that the bass angler does, and trout lures are generally smaller.

I like a plastic tackle box. It doesn't rust, requires a minimum of maintenance, and isn't noisy. I want the smallest box that will accommodate my tackle, but it should have sturdy hinges and clasps that won't let it pop open and spill my tackle.

Even the stream fisherman, who rarely takes a tackle box to trout

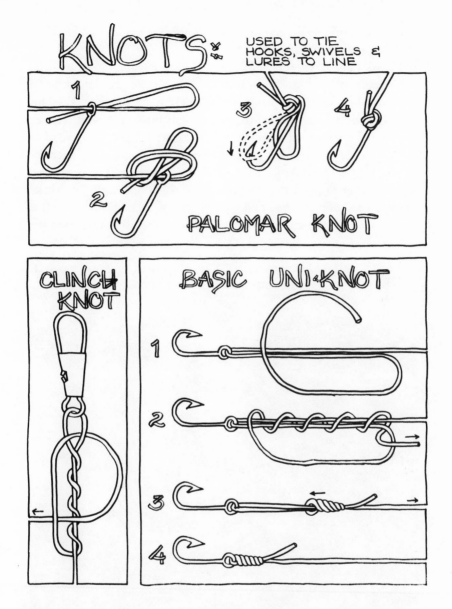

These knots can safely be used for tying lures to monofilament line.

waters, will find one handy for storing the wide assortment of tackle and keeping it organized.

If you believe there's nothing quite like wading a stream, you need some other means for carrying your tackle. Various kinds of shoulder bags are good, and many creels have extra pockets for storing gear. My choice for stream fishing is the fishing vest. I credit the fly fishermen for its invention. But regardless of your mode of fishing, a fishing vest is one of the handiest items you can own. While it apparently is an item of clothing, it has little functional value in that respect. It does little for your comfort, provides little warmth, and doesn't shed rain.

I prefer a vest to a fishing jacket because I can wear my vest over

A fishing vest with many pockets for odds and ends of tackle is handy. Most vests also have a built-in creel across the back. Photo by Pat Gooch

whatever clothing the weather dictates. I even wear it over my bare skin if the weather is hot and muggy.

A good vest has many roomy pockets, most of which can be closed by zippers, snaps, or buttons to prevent the loss of tackle. Look for loops for attaching landing nets, fish stringers, and other equipment that should be at your fingertips. And I want my vest to have a big ventilated creel across the back.

If the weather is cool enough, I use the vest's creel for my catch. But in warm weather, I prefer to string the fish through both lips and let them trail in the water behind me.

In order to best utilize a fishing vest, you should buy plastic boxes to fit the pockets. Boxes are handy for storing various items you'll need on the stream. By contrast, long-nosed pliers for removing lures—and nail clippers for cutting line—should be tied to your vest and left dangling for ready use.

Many trout are lost between the water and the boat or creel. It is a critical time, and care must be used to prevent loss of a prize. Some anglers scoff at landing nets, but a good one will save you many a lightly hooked trout. The boat angler can afford the luxury of a big boat net with a long handle, but the wading angler will need a smaller one with a short handle. You can secure it to your vest or sling it over your shoulder on an elastic cord that will stretch when you reach for a trout.

For outsized trout, a gaff may be necessary, but a landing net will handle most situations.

When you fish from a boat you can keep your catch fresh in a live box, on a stringer, or in a bag fastened to the side of your boat. Live boxes are ideal, but not all boats have them. A metal-chain stringer, plastic coated for quietness, that can be lowered over the side will also keep trout alive and fresh. In hot weather, it might be a good idea to attach an extension and lower the fish deep in the water—out of the warm surface water. If you can't keep your fish alive, your best bet is to kill them immediately and place them in a chest on ice.

Many wading anglers prefer the time-tested willow creel. It's traditional and still tops. The air circulates freely through such a creel, and wet grass or ferns can be used to help keep your catch fresh.

Regardless of where you do your trout fishing, you should have a good assortment of sinkers. If you cast small wet flies to headwater trout, you'll need tiny split-shot sinkers that clamp onto the line. They *can* damage the line, so care should be exercised and the line tested once split-shots are in place to make certain it has not been weakened. Those with the little tabs on the back to facilitate their removal are my choice. A good selection of split-shot sinkers in a variety of weights will handle most trout-fishing situations. I like to carry a few clincher, slip, and rubber-core sinkers. Keel sinkers for trolling plus a small assortment of dipsey sinkers should round out the spinning trouter's needs.

Many hardy anglers simply wade wet, as Aaron F. Pass does here in Georgia's Chattahoochee River. He takes time from his fishing to explain a spinning technique to a young angler he met on the stream.

"I like natural baits for high water or cold weather when the trout are sluggish," one veteran of many trout seasons once told me. This good advice calls for a selection of sharp fishhooks. For the wide variety of trout fishing available across the United States and Canada, anglers need a good variety of hook sizes. Turned-down eyes are usually the best for baitfishing, but straight shanks are better for trolling minnows and other baits. Short-shanked hooks are best for fishing salmon eggs, corn, and the various cheese baits.

The best hooks are made of high-quality tempered steel and will bend before they break.

A trout's mouth is not hard to drive a hook into, but the point should be sharp. If it is not, either sharpen the dull one or discard it and tie on another. A small file or stone will be necessary.

Tiny gold-colored hooks are the choice of the great majority of fishermen who dunk corn, eggs, or worms for hatchery-reared trout that rarely exceed a pound. A good selection of hook sizes would include some 8, 6, 4, 2, and 1s for smaller trout and a few 1/0, 2/0, and 3/0 sizes for outsized fish.

Most trout fishermen are stream waders, for in much of our trout country the bulk of the hatchery trout are stocked in streams, though ponds and lakes get a few. Your chances of success on a stream are enhanced considerably if you wade. To do so comfortably, you need hip boots or waders, which are also handy for wading the shallows of ponds and lakes.

Chest waders are my usual choice. They permit me to cover a greater variety of waters, and I do not risk going in over my boot tops, as I have done in hip boots. Chest waders are warmer in cold weather, and in a downpour I can drop a rain shirt over my head and keep completely dry. If you do much cold-weather fishing, your waders should be insulated. But in most fishing, regular waders worn over heavy socks will keep your feet warm.

Hip boots are less expensive and a good choice for warm weather. Some anglers even wade wet during warm weather. I prefer boots —not only to keep dry but also because they protect my feet against rocks and other underwater objects.

When you must hike a long distance to reach remote trout waters, waders or hip boots are cumbersome. For this situation I prefer light stockingfoot waders that come to the waist and are held in

Chest waders are the choice of most anglers who wade when fishing streams or the shallows of ponds and lakes. A belt around the waist will help prevent water from pouring into the waders should the angler fall. Here the author fishes the Gravel Pit Lakes in New Mexico. Photo by Ginny Gooch

place by an elastic waistband. Over these waders I wear ordinary tennis shoes, though regular ankle-height wading shoes would be better. The waders pack into a tiny package that is easy to carry on a long hike into the backcountry.

Floats or bobbers play minor roles in spinning for trout, but there are occasions when they come in handy. The most popular float is a plastic ball with a wire hook that holds the line in place. A spring-controlled plunger facilitates attaching the bobber to a line and removing it. Most are red and white for high visibility, but other color combinations are available in most tackle shops. Clear-plastic floats are available for use with dry flies on light spinning tackle, the only means of fishing dry flies on such tackle.

"I fish spinning tackle with a plastic float and dry flies most of the time," said Steve Martinez recently when we were discussing trout fishing on the Jicarilla Apache Indian Reservation in New Mexico, where he works as a conservation officer.

Other floats have holes in the middle through which the line is run. This type of float is held in place with a wedge that fits into the hole. These bobbers are usually of plastic, also; some are made of cork.

Most floats are spherical, but some are bullet shaped to offer less resistance when a trout hits the bait and moves away with it. For extremely delicate situations—where the slightest resistance of a float might cause a wary trout to drop the bait—porcupine quills are useful. They offer a minimum of resistance, but they will support a baited hook at the desired depth.

Floats are handy for baitfishing when you must suspend a live minnow or other natural bait at the depth the trout are feeding. They are also useful for suspending bait just above aquatic vegetation to keep the bait from becoming buried in the grass or weeds.

On strange lakes and large rivers, the electronic fish finder is helpful in reading the water. It will not only indicate the location of fish but will also help you find dropoffs, bars, brushpiles, and other kinds of underwater structures. In the absence of such a gadget, your best bet is to get a contour map of the lake or stream to help you unravel some of its secrets. Doing so is essential to successful fishing.

Where trout regulations impose minimum-size limits, you need some means of measuring the fish. The DeLiar is popular. It has a small scale for weighing fish, and a spring-controlled ruler that winds into the body of the device when not in use. Many creels have rulers on them, or you can devise your own—on the butt of your fishing rod, creel, or tackle box.

Long-nosed pliers have many uses: for reaching deep into the trout's mouth to free a hook or lure, to clamp onto or remove sinkers, and for various other purposes. Some anglers prefer surgical hemostats, which serve the same purpose. Ordinary nail clippers come in handy for snipping lures off lines or trimming loose ends of line or leaders. So clippers should be in every tackle box or fishing vest.

A quick check of my tackle box also turns up a small pair of scissors (though the nail clippers make them less essential) and a small screwdriver for emergency repairs. There is also a can of reel oil, a small hone for sharpening dull hooks, sunglasses for eye comfort, and, as an aid in seeing below the water's surface, a Boy Scout knife that contains a sharp blade, screwdriver, punch, and can opener. I also carry a small towel for drying my hands after I have handled a fish.

These items make up the basic tackle, and there is some overlapping of functions. But that is better than not having something you need. Personal preferences may cause you to add other odds and ends of tackle.

Just owning all the right gear, though, is not enough.

"My tackle box is a mess," muttered a fishing partner recently as he fumbled for something he could not find.

The real secret is to keep all of your gear organized.

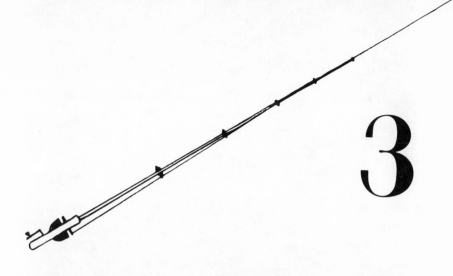

3

The Cast and the Strike

Of the various forms of casting (baitcasting, flycasting, and spinning) the cast with spinning tackle is by far the easiest to master. This characteristic plus a great versatility has made spinning the most popular form of angling in America today. And the wonder is that it has reached this status in a few short years.

Actually, there are three—possibly four—basic spinning casts that will enable you to handle just about any problem you encounter on the trout stream or lake. They are: (1) the overhand-cast (the basic one), (2) the side-cast, (3) the underhand-cast, and (4) the bow-and-arrow cast. The bow-and-arrow cast has very limited application.

The conventional and most popular delivery is the overhand-cast. It will handle most fishing situations, and it's the first one most beginners get the knack of. For lake or big-water fishing, there is seldom a need for any other kind of cast.

The overhand-cast begins with the tip of the rod pointed at the

The author touches the line with his index finger as he completes a cast and lowers the rod tip while fishing for cutthroat trout on Boulder Creek in Idaho.

target (the spot you want your lure to hit) with approximately six inches of line between the rod tip and the lure. From this position, bring the rod tip sharply upward to a point just to the rear of your shoulder. Then snap the rod quickly forward and release the line when the rod is at approximately a 45-degree angle to your body. Most of the power comes from your wrist.

There are two generally recognized variations of the overhand-cast: (1) the *snap*-cast I've just described, and (2) the softer *swinging*-cast. The snap-cast is used primarily for artificial lures; the swinging-cast is best when you're fishing natural baits.

The soft-cast begins much the same way with the rod tip pointed at the target. But you swing the rod back more slowly and make a deeper back-cast. Instead of snapping the rod forward—a move almost certain to snap off the bait—you swing it forward as softly as possible.

The soft-cast can also be used when the lure is heavier than normal. The snap-cast, however, is best accomplished with a fast-taper rod and well-balanced tackle—rod, reel, and line.

Whereas the snap-cast is accomplished mostly by action of the wrist, the soft-cast is delivered more by the forearm and with limited wrist action.

A common mistake made by beginners is to bring the rod tip too far back on the back-cast and then release the line too quickly on the forward-cast. The result is an arching cast that may send the lure into overhanging branches. A good way to iron out such kinks in casting form is to practice in your backyard while a fishing partner observes and suggests corrections.

The overhand-cast is ideal on big bodies of water. There are few overhead obstructions, and the target is open water that's free of obstacles.

When you fish small streams, you'll seldom enjoy ideal casting conditions. Usually, you're either wading beneath overhanging

The side-cast is a modification of the conventional overhand-cast. It can be used to get lure or bait back beneath overhanging vegetation. The conventional overhand cast is generally limited to lakes and ponds and open water on streams.

branches that limit your casting space or you're trying to place your lure or bait far back beneath overhanging vegetation. Under such conditions, the overhand-cast will not work.

The side-cast is the answer to such problems. On many streams, you find yourself employing this cast, or variations of it, more than you use the conventional overhand-cast. The side-cast is also good on windy days when you want to keep your lure close to the surface of the water—out of the wind.

In close quarters, you may have to resort to a backhand-cast. In this variation, you first bring your casting hand to approximately the point of your opposite shoulder. Then you cast by swinging your arm *away* from your chest. The maneuver resembles a backhand stroke in tennis.

Accuracy is difficult when you use the side-cast. The usual tendency is to release the line too quickly on the forward-cast, sending the lure or bait off target. Practice will help.

Occasionally, you'll have no room for even the side-cast. Then the underhand (or pendulum) cast can provide some accuracy in placing the lure in a tight spot. This cast involves little more than holding the rod horizontally and swinging the lure back and forth beneath the rod tip until it gets enough momentum to release it toward the target on a forward swing. Most fishermen, at some time during their careers, have fished with cane poles, swinging a line on the long pole to place a baited hook in the desired spot. The underhand-cast with the spinning rod is much the same, except that you can achieve greater distance.

The bow-and-arrow cast can be used to shoot a lure into an otherwise inaccessible spot. To do so, point the rod tip at the target and grasp the lure in your left hand (if you're right-handed). Pull the lure back, bending the rod tip downward. When there is a good bend in the rod, release the lure, permitting the power of the rod to shoot it toward the target. A word of caution: *Grasp the lure so that all points and barbs are forward of your grip so they cannot sink into your fingers on the release.*

Mastery of these few forms of casting will enable you to cover just about any kind of trout water you encounter.

Over the years, I have picked up a few tricks that help iron out kinks in casting form.

A common mistake is to attempt too long a cast. It is much more effective to move within easy casting range and maintain control than to cast from far back and develop sloppy habits while trying vainly to reach a target. You occasionally may have to sacrifice accuracy for distance. Usually, however, this need occurs only on large bodies of water where accuracy is less important than it is on small streams.

Steve Aleshi, a national distance-casting champion, says he gets additional casting distance by rearing back like a baseball pitcher and accelerating on the forward cast. He puts the most power into the last foot and a half of arm motion.

Unlike the baitcaster, the spinning angler does not have to transfer the rod from the casting hand to the other hand when the lure hits the water. You can begin your retrieve a split second sooner, if necessary.

How quickly you begin your retrieve depends upon a number of factors. Usually, trout are near the bottom of the lake or stream, so you must give the lure time to sink. But in shallow water, the retrieve must be started almost immediately.

When trout are feeding on or near the surface, as they may be early or late in the day, the lure should be worked shallow. As a spinning angler, however, you're at a disadvantage when trout are feeding on the top. That's when the fly fisherman has a decided edge.

In spinning for trout, you'll rarely use surface lures. But when you do, you should give the water a chance to settle before you start your retrieve. The ripples from the cast should fade away. A surface cast may spook the trout temporarily. Trout tend to give a surface lure a more critical look.

The position of the rod is important on the retrieve. When you fish with artificial lures, the tip should be held low to allow plenty of striking room.

With most natural baits, however, the trout should be permitted to run a bit, and too much line tension may warn the fish. In that situation, the rod tip should be held high so it can be dropped when the trout strikes. This tactic provides immediate slack. If more slack is needed, you have time to flip open the bail—if it is not open—so the line will peel off.

THE CAST AND THE STRIKE

Long casts are rarely necessary to take trout, particularly in stream fishing. Actually, it is better to make short casts and move frequently. Short casts not only are more accurate but also can be dropped on the water more softly. And in clear water, you can often see the fish hit on a short cast, and you can react more quickly. On a short line, you can fight the fish better. The long line may develop a belly that makes it hard to set the hook quickly, and the stretching quality of monofilament is more troublesome on a long line. With a long line out, you have less control over a fighting trout and may experience difficulty keeping it away from snags and other obstacles.

When you get a hit on artificial lures, you should strike sharply. This maneuver is of less importance when fishing natural baits. Trout often take natural baits deep in their throats, so setting the hook is not so crucial.

Light (two- to four-pound-test) monofilament line and soft-action rods make striking difficult. So you must strike hard to compensate for these weaknesses. On a short line, the sharp upward flick of your wrist will set a hook. But on long lines, you must get your entire body into the action. By using only sharp hooks, you will help ensure a high percentage of connections on striking trout. A trout's mouth is much softer than that of many another gamefish.

Playing a trout can be a critical time in fishing, especially if the fish leaps frequently, as does the rainbow. To protect the line, set the reel's drag adjustment just below the breaking point of the line. This precaution, plus the flexibility of the rod, should limit the risk that a trout will break even a two-pound-test line.

There is no way to avoid losing a few trout, but maintaining a tight line will help.

Some anglers point their rods almost directly at the fish during the battle, but this practice does not take advantage of the play in the rod. The give and take of a lively rod tip will soon tire a trout. To gain this advantage, hold the rod near the ten-o'clock position. Some experienced anglers hold their rods even higher.

When a trout leaps, many anglers like to slap the rod toward the surface of the water, but maintaining a tight line is more critical.

Many anglers pump big trout by dropping the rod tip, reeling in line as they do so, and working the fish in by gently raising the rod

As he retrieves a lure in a likely stretch of the Williams River in West Virginia, the author keeps the rod tip low. Photo by Pat Gooch

to the ten-o'clock position. They then repeat the process. It is a method borrowed from saltwater anglers who go after big fish.

Most trout are lost either within moments after they strike or when being landed. Those lost early in the fight are lightly hooked, often in the very edge of the lip, and the angler is beaten before he even begins the battle. At the net, many trout are lost because an overanxious angler attempts to land a "green" trout, one still full of fight.

The best way to safely land a good trout is to play it carefully and continue the fight until the fish is exhausted. A tired trout will turn on its side. That's your signal that the trout is ready for the net or gaff.

In order to take advantage of rod flexibility, you should hold the

rod high, at the eleven-o'clock position or higher. Leave plenty of line out. This tactic will prevent a tired trout from lunging in a final bid for freedom and snapping the line. The trout's head should be kept up and out of the water if possible. You thereby neutralize the power left in its fins and tail.

Most trout are landed by netting. The best approach is to gently slide the net's mouth beneath the trout and then scoop it up quickly. Use of the gaff is riskier. With a swift stroke, drive the gaff into the fish behind its gills and swing it quickly out of the water.

Some stream fishermen refuse to use a net, and they occasionally pay with the loss of a fish. If you don't have a net, work the trout as close to a sandbar or sloping bank as you can and then scoot it quickly ashore with a fast swing of your rod. Big trout can be hauled ashore by hand. Grasp the trout firmly just ahead of the tail. In the jargon of the angler, this is known as tailing the fish.

The more you fish with your spinning tackle, the more you will learn about its versatility and the ways it can be used successfully in the art of trouting.

Netting is the safest way to land a trout. Here the author prepares to net one on the Bullpasture River in Virginia.

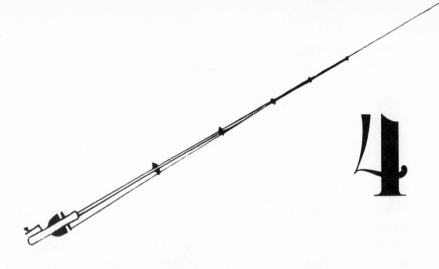

The Lures

When you're spinning for trout, you use tackle that's so flexible it can be used with a wide variety of lures. In fact, every trout lure in America can be fished on spinning tackle, and so can most bass lures, pike lures, walleye lures, and many others. Some of these possibilities are more effective and more adaptable to spinning than others, and many have dubious value as trout lures.

I was opening one season on South River, a popular trout stream that races off the eastern slopes of the Blue Ridge Mountains in western Virginia. The stream was crowded, the water high, and the weather colder than usual for opening day. Natural bait was indicated, but the action was slow.

"Think I'll try something else," I told my fishing partner.

I went back to the car, traded my worm can for a tiny box of spinning lures, and walked a considerable distance downstream—to get away from the crowd.

Deep down I didn't really expect much success and my first cast was almost automatic. But then I took up the slack in the monofilament and began to work the tiny spinner–fly combination lure across the fast current. A trout hit, and I came wide awake. With a flick of my wrist, I set the hook, and a twelve-inch rainbow split the surface of the icy water. I worked the fish carefully to the net. When I cast again, it was with renewed enthusiasm.

Methodically and slowly, I worked my way back upstream: through big holes lined with worming anglers and through the fast riffles. Eventually, as other anglers headed for home, I had the stream almost to myself.

Late in the afternoon and far upstream, I took my eighth trout, a fat brookie, from a deep hole where baitfishermen had already landed a dozen or so trout. I filled my limit.

"The flexibility of your spinning tackle allowed you to make that successful change of tactics," my partner observed as we drove happily home.

The Spinner–Fly Combination Lures

At the top of my list of spinning lures are the small spinner–fly combinations produced by a number of tackle companies. Among my favorites are the Mepps, Panther/Martins, Roostertails, and Shysters, but the variety and sizes are almost unlimited.

The spinner–fly combination features a spinner, a shaft to which the spinner is attached, often several bright beads on the shaft, and a hook behind the spinner. The hook is trimmed with hair or feathers. Most manufacturers also offer lures with just the hook, beads, and blades.

On the conventional spinner–fly lure, the hook rides directly behind the spinner. But the success of bass anglers in recent years with the spinnerbait (on which the blade is offset) has influenced manufacturers of the spinner–fly trout lures. Both Mepps and Roostertail lures are now available in this style. The spinner rides near the point of the hook on a shaft that runs diagonally off the main stem. Such a lure avoids more weeds and snags than do conventional lures, so these little spinnerbaits are good in debris-laden waters.

A spinner–fly combination lure attracted this nice rainbow trout from Cheoah Lake in North Carolina. Photo by Bill Nichols

A spinner–fly combination lure usually has a single spinner blade, but the blade shape can vary widely. The narrow, willow-leaf blade is best for fast water, where the pressure of the current will cause it to spin. But in quiet water, such as lakes and ponds, a broad blade is usually necessary to get enough action from the lure.

For streams where trout will average ten to twelve inches, I like the small lures; sizes 0 or 1 in Mepps, for example. If the size of the fish dictates it, however, I go to sizes 2 or 3 or larger.

On my workbench is a lure-making kit produced by the Worth Fishing Tackle Company. In it are the spoons, hooks, beads, swivels, weights, and paint for assembling twenty-five spinning lures—if I ever find the time to do so. Many anglers build their own lures.

While the variety of spinning lures seems endless and new ones appear with every fishing season, lures of value to trout anglers can be grouped generally into spinners, spoons, plugs, jigs, flies, and streamers.

Spinners

The spinners get a lot of attention from trout fishermen. The various spinner–fly combinations are popular, and a similar lure can be fashioned by combining regular spinners with flies or streamers. Generally, however, anglers prefer to use the assembled lures such as the Roostertails and Shysters.

Regular spinners come with one or two blades and can be used in combination with a great variety of lures from worms and other natural baits to streamers and wet flies.

The spinner revolves on a straight shaft that has an eye at one end for fastening to the leader or line. On the shaft's other end is a snap, for attaching a hook or fly. Since the eyes of many flies or streamers are tiny—designed for light monofilament—the snap on the spinner shaft may be too large in diameter for them. So it's a good idea to stock a few spinners assembled on thin wire for threading through the tiny eyes. The eyes of most bare hooks, however, are large enough to accommodate the snap on the average spinner shaft.

Trout-catching combinations of spinners, hooks, baits, and lures are almost endless and many are overlooked.

Spinners that do not spin are worthless. To make sure they work, polish the shafts with fine steel wool and then oil them very lightly.

Casting weight can be a problem with regular spinners because the combined weight of the spinner, the thin shaft, and the average fly or streamer isn't heavy enough to cast effectively. Natural baits such as minnows and night crawlers may add the necessary weight, but ordinarily the angler must add casting weight. I like split-shot sinkers. They can be clamped onto the shaft of the spinner or onto the line six to twelve inches above the spinner. Make sure the sinker won't hamper the action. Check the action by pulling the lure through the water nearby and watching.

On most eastern waters, the smallest spinner available is big enough. The 0 size is a good choice. On the big western rivers, however, a size 3 or 2 might be more appropriate, though most anglers will use smaller ones if they can.

High and cloudy water usually calls for a fairly large spinner. Spinners with gold blades are usually good for summer stream fishing, but in high, roily water the blades should be of fluorescent color. When the sun is bright and the water low and clear, gold or copper spinners are a good choice. Even black, green, or red ones are good then. They attract the trout without blinding them with the flash of silver.

To get a spinner deep in the current of a stream, you have a choice of several techniques. When you want to get your spinner deep for a spot you expect a trout to be holding, cast a good distance upstream from the spot. The spinner will sink rapidly as it moves with the current, much more quickly than will a fly or streamer. Dropping the spinner into an undercurrent will also get it down to the desired depth. A spinner will usually sink when you cast it upstream, but on a downstream cast you must allow slack in the line for the spinner to sink.

Spoons

All kinds of fish—including trout—are taken on spoons in various sizes and shapes. Spoons are age-old and well-tested fishing lures, and a great variety have been built for spinning tackle. My tackle box contains a good selection of colors, shapes, and sizes, and they all get used.

Most spoons are solid, one-piece lures with treble hooks. Some, though, are altered to include tiny little tabs that flash and flutter for additional appeal.

Many veteran anglers consider the spoon the most versatile and consistent of all trout lures. There is no better testimonial to the spoon than the fact that most survival kits contain a small selection. People who know their trout fishing realize that when the chips are down, spoons will usually do the trick. A good selection of colors, shapes, sizes, and weights is almost a guarantee of trout-fishing success. All can be fished on spinning tackle.

This nice Saskatchewan lake trout went for a spoon trolled on spinning tackle.

Spoons resemble minnows or baitfish, a staple in some trout diets. But trout will hit spoons even in high mountain lakes that have nothing resembling such food.

Spoons are often called wobblers because of their peculiar side-to-side action when worked slowly. Do not be confused by the variation in language.

Like spinners, some spoons are broad-beamed, while others are narrow and resemble willow leaves. Both spoon types have their places in the plans of the complete trout fisherman. The broad and usually light spoons are good for fishing the quiet waters of a lake or pond. They need a minimum of movement to provide good action, and they usually run close to the surface. For deep fishing, or for fishing in streams with a strong current, the narrower and heavier willow-leaf spoons are a better choice.

Most spoons have treble hooks, but sometimes single hooks are better. You'll do better with single hooks in water filled with debris, grass, or weeds. Some spoons come with a single hook, and you can always substitute a single hook for the treble ones. The effect on the action is slight.

Weight is important in the selection of a spoon, and the numerous imitations of name brands on the market today are sometimes questionable in this respect. They are usually lighter than the lure they imitate. This difference can cause a casting problem.

The classic red-and-white spoon is a good choice for trout fishing, but spoons with scalelike finishes are also good. Sometimes nothing is quite so effective as the plain silver spoon, which probably looks like a shiner to the hungry trout. I like a variety of colors in my selection: red, orange, yellow, green, blue, and violet. Perch and other patterns should also be included.

Usually a sparkling spoon will take more trout than a dark one, but not always. When the water is low and clear, a dark one may work best.

For trout in the eight- to twelve-inch range, use spoons in the three-fourth- to one-inch size. But if trout in the fifteen-inch or larger size are expected, step up to a few one- to two-inchers.

Since the advent of spinning tackle, spinners, spoons, and other lures built for flyrod use have become almost a thing of the past, but those tiny spoons can work wonders. Fish them on ultralight spinning tackle. I own several fingernail-size spoons that were produced with the flyrod in mind, but I take trout on them with my ultralight spinning tackle.

Spoons can be a nuisance to pack because they tend to tangle. Some anglers solve this problem by removing the hooks from all of their spoons and packing the hooks and spoons in separate compartments. Since hooks are connected to the better spoons with split rings, it's a simple matter to attach the size and type of hook you prefer to the spoon of your choice. Split-ring pliers should be packed for this purpose.

The spoon can be the most important lure in the trout angler's tackle box.

Plugs

Plugs see little action on American trout waters, but I recall one cold opening day when I used a flyrod-size Flatfish. The lure has good action, and on that April day, the trout seemed to prefer it over all else.

"When trout show a preference, I accommodate them," I tell new anglers.

Plugs can imitate a host of aquatic citizens: minnows, frogs, tadpoles, crayfish, and even mice and baby ducks. The trout angler will usually fare best, however, with plugs that imitate minnows.

Even bass-size plugs can be brought into use for large trout, but then you must use a heavy (six- to eight-ounce) rod and matching reel and line. The great majority of plugs on the market today were designed for bass and other warm-water fish such as pike and muskie. Very few were designed for trout.

"A rainbow trout!" exclaimed Walt Skidmore as he worked a thrashing fish to the boat. Walt and I were fishing West Virginia's Summersville Lake for bass when the flashy rainbow hit his plug. Summersville is one of West Virginia's best trout lakes, and the bass fishing is also good.

The variety of available plugs is rich. Plugs are designed to fish deep, shallow, or on the surface. I have never heard of anyone fishing for trout with surface plugs, but I will not say it has not been done successfully. I'm sure an artificial mouse worked seductively on the surface of a quiet brown-trout hole would induce a savage strike from the big brown that rules the pool.

Jigs or Doll Flies

The jig or doll fly is another lure that will take trout, but it gets limited use on most trout waters. The jig is a heavy lead-head lure with a single hook usually dressed with deer hair, feathers, or chenille. In recent years, soft plastic has come into use on some lures in lieu of hair, feathers, or chenille. The result is a highly effective lure, one that will take just about any trout.

All types of jigs come in various colors, but the plastic ones offer the greatest variety.

This giant Tennessee brown trout went for a Rebel plug. Photo by Tennessee Wildlife Resources Agency

Jigs also come in a great variety of weights, and they all cast like bullets on properly matched tackle. The smallest ones, those ranging in weight from one-thirty-second to one-fourth ounce, are usually best for trout. Generally, the trout angler will have little use for the larger sizes.

Lead-head jigs are available in a variety of patterns. The shape of heads can vary tremendously, and they are dressed with a variety of feathers, hair, plastics, and rubber. The conventional spherical or bullet heads are good choices for stream fishing for trout, but the bullet head is less likely to snag.

One highly effective lure for the big brook trout is a hair-dressed jig with a short section of plastic worm on the hook, fished in conjunction with a spinner. This combination should be allowed to sink to the bottom before being retrieved.

Just recently, the value of the jig was again brought home to me. I was fishing for hatchery-reared trout on the Hughes River, a delightful little stream that races eastward through the Virginia foothills. The opening-day water was a bit high. Because the stream was crowded, I elected to use worms on light spinning tackle. I quickly took a couple of trout, and then the action fell off.

A fellow angler was having better luck on cheese, a bait I never fish, but I dug into my tackle bag and found a small yellow jig that was a fair imitation of cheese. It matched my ultralight spinning tackle.

I tied on the jig and made a cast into the current, letting the lure roll downstream. At the end of the drift, my line tightened and the lure swung out of the current. A good trout hit, and I set the hook. Almost immediately, a nice rainbow rocketed out of the icy water, clearing the surface by a good two feet. Who says those hatchery trout don't fight?

I hung on as the fish leaped again, and this time the lure flew loose when the trout hit the water.

I reeled in and cast again. I had the answer to the cheese bait.

The jig has absolutely no built-in action other than that provided by the dressing, and that's not much. For stream fishing, where the current rolls the lure downstream, action is unnecessary. But in the quiet waters of a lake or pond, you need to give the lure some action. One way is to retrieve the jig sporadically, permitting it to sink rapidly between spurts.

Wet Flies and Streamers

Any wet fly or streamer can be fished on spinning tackle. Just add a one-sixteenth-ounce split-shot sinker six inches above the lure to provide the needed casting weight.

The basic fly colors are black, brown, gray, and light cream.

A good selection of fly patterns should include the Adams, Black Gnat, Blue Dun, Brown Hackle, Coachman, Gold Ribbed Hare's Ear, Quill Gordon, Gray Hackle, Hendrickson, Leadwing Coachman, Light Cahill, Light Hendrickson, Royal Coachman, Silver

Doctor, and the Sulfur Dun. With these, you're equipped to fish anywhere in North America, and you can fish these wet flies and streamers on spinning tackle, sometimes better than you can on traditional fly tackle.

Sizes 6, 8, and 10 will fit most occasions, but it's wise to add a few larger ones and a few tiny 12 and 14 sizes.

Good streamer patterns include the Black Nose Dace, Mickey Finn, and Muddler Minnow.

One of my favorite kinds of trout fishing is to go after the tiny native brook trout high in the Blue Ridge Mountains or the Alleghenies. For years I fished fly tackle exclusively on these little streams, but casting room is generally limited. Space for a back-cast is almost nonexistent, and often a cast is little more than swinging the line much as you would the baited hook on a cane pole.

And then along came ultralight spinning tackle and an easy solution to my casting problem. The tiny little rods of five feet or less, one- or two-pound-test lines, and watch-size reels seemed to be just the thing for these crowded streams.

On my next trip to the mountains, my flyrod stayed home. In its place went a delicate ultralight spinning outfit. A tiny split-shot about six inches above the fly gave me all the casting weight I needed. There was no back-cast problem, and I experienced little trouble dropping the fly anywhere I wanted to in the sparkling little stream. The trout responded magnificently.

Any wet fly or streamer can be fished in this manner, and you are certainly not restricted to those little headwaters streams. The possibilities are limited only by your imagination.

To take trout during the summer and fall, try the various grasshopper imitations such as Joe's Hopper, the Michigan Hopper, or the Muddler. They are often productive in big waters that meander through open meadows, and they're especially good on windy days when the trout are alert for grasshoppers blown into the stream.

Western-steelhead flies such as the Thor and Atomic are good on eastern trout streams in the spring. When weighted, they will sink rapidly and can be retrieved erratically along the bottom. Big flies or lures are often the answer in the spring when the water is high.

Streamers, highly productive lures for just about all of the trouts, can be fished in this same way.

When selecting a streamer, some anglers first try to determine what kind of minnows inhabit the water. They then attempt to imitate them.

On the large rivers, a three-inch streamer is a good size to start with. If it doesn't produce, drop to a two-inch size. These streamers are usually tied on size 4 to 6 hooks. Even a four-inch streamer might work at times. It is usually tied on a size 2 to 1/0 hook.

Streamers should generally be fished deep—on or near the bottom. A split-shot six inches above the lure will get them down. Some anglers prefer lead strips that can be wrapped around the line.

A dark (color) streamer is often a good choice for a bright day. Dull (finish) ones may also be good. But on dark, overcast days, the light, bright streamers will usually produce better. The bright ones are also often best early in the morning and late in the afternoon, when the light is dim.

Light, brightly colored streamers are also good when the water is roily, but the somber-colored ones are best for clear waters. A brightly colored streamer or lure is also more effective when the water and weather are cold.

Streamers, when cast upstream, will sink well and can be fished deep. They should be retrieved in darts and spurts to imitate a crippled minnow.

In addition to the ones already mentioned, good streamer patterns include the Doctor Oatman, Gray Smelt, Male Dace, Parmacheene Belle, Sanborn, Silver Darter, and Miracle Marabou.

Dry Flies

Dry flies on spinning tackle are not as effective as streamers and wet flies, but dries can be cast with a plastic bubble or float to add casting weight.

"I fish mostly with dry flies and a float on spinning tackle," Steve Martinez of the Jicarilla Apache tribe of northern New Mexico told me recently as we prepared to fish Embon Lake on the tribe's reservation. Martinez, a tribe conservation officer, outfished me as I stuck with the more conventional lures for the scrappy rainbow trout.

Dry flies are at the bottom of my list for catching trout, however, and I seldom fish them. When conditions dictate the use of dry flies, I prefer to switch to a flyrod and enjoy some of the finest trout fishing available.

Still, I keep a plastic bubble and a few dry flies in my spinning kit for times that dry flies are needed and a flyrod is unavailable.

Despite its versatility, spinning tackle is at its best when used with the wide variety of lures designed just for spinning. They are made of metal, wood, rubber, plastic, feathers, hair, and glue, and the only limit on combinations is the imagination of the lure manufacturer, whether commercial or individual.

And your imagination is about the only limit on the various lures or lure combinations that can be fished on spinning tackle. Learn to experiment.

The spinning angler should never overlook his ability to fish tiny lures. That is a major advantage. When you go to heavy lures, you're in one sense defeating the purpose of your tackle.

Browse through the lure department of any large tackle shop and note the great variety of lures—plastic imitations of frogs and minnows and soft plastic worms in a great variety of sizes, shapes, and colors. Most worms are intended for bass, but trout will hit the right plastic worms fished seductively on spinning tackle.

The trout fisherman who is willing to use his imagination and experiment is usually the most successful one. Spinning tackle favors such an imagination.

5

Natural Baits

I took my first trout, a hatchery-reared brookie, on a worm, the garden variety dug that morning from moist earth warming slowly beneath a spring sun. I suspect most trout fishermen of my generation did likewise. If they were easterners, chances are good that their first trout was a brookie; if they started fishing in the west, their first trout may well have been a cutthroat or a rainbow.

I fished that early worm on a battered bamboo rod, the accepted bait rod around my way before the advent of spinning tackle.

Having been so introduced to trout fishing, and having tingled with joy for hours after that first encounter with the brilliantly colored brookie, I give the worm a special place in my memory.

Aside from its nostalgic value, the worm has a place in the plans of most trout fishermen. Early in the season when the waters are high, cold, and tainted, the worm can salvage a trout-fishing trip.

To many modern trout fishermen, bait means corn, cheese,

salmon eggs, marshmallows, and the like. Most of these baits will take hatchery trout, but not necessarily native brook trout. The lowly worm, often referred to as garden hackle, is highly effective on native brook trout, and also on other trout.

Worms

There is something fundamentally satisfying about taking trout on natural baits, and I get almost as much pleasure from digging into the good earth for worms as I do from the fishing. Digging worms is part of the opening-day ritual, something that signals the beginning of a bright new fishing season.

Usually by opening day across trout country the earth has thawed and warmed enough for you to collect worms. Look for garden plots, particularly old ones that have been heavily fertilized over a number of years—or even old abandoned ones. Rich soil around barns is noted for producing healthy worms.

I have a handy area in my backyard where I collect worms. Each day when I feed my dogs I take fresh droppings out of the kennel and pile them nearby for periodic removal. Over the years, the droppings have fertilized that soil so richly that I can find worms within a few inches of the surface.

Worms can also be gathered by turning over rocks, rotting boards, or other timber where the soil is fertile.

If the earth is still frozen when the trout season opens, or there is no convenient place to collect worms, then your best bet is a nearby tackle shop. Most offer a choice of worms: red wigglers or night crawlers. For most trout fishing, I prefer red wigglers. They're near ideal for the small trout hooks. But night crawlers might be a better choice for the larger trout in lakes and rivers. (Night crawlers, incidentally, can be gathered by walking a well-fertilized golf course or lawn at night and searching the grass with a flashlight.)

To keep worms alive and kicking, saturate a sheet of newspaper in water, remove it, let it drip a few minutes, and then place it in a cardboard container. Scatter the worms loosely over the sheet of newspaper, and place another saturated sheet on top of them. The worms should be stored overnight in a cool place (around 45°F.) if possible. They will be good and lively for the next day's fishing.

Worms are a natural bait for brook trout, especially during a spring runoff or after a heavy rain. Some anglers prefer night crawlers because they can be cast on light spinning tackle without added weight, but even garden worms can be cast on ultralight spinning tackle without added weight.

The unweighted worm drifts naturally, and it does not hang up as quickly as a weighted one.

When you fish streams, cast the worm upstream, well above the spot you intend to fish. By the time the worm drifts downstream, it will be tumbling naturally near the bottom. The bail on your spinning reel should remain open, and you control the line with your fingers.

A worm trailing behind a couple of small Indiana spinners can also be deadly on a spinning rod. A spinner or two gives the worm additional casting weight.

For most fishing, hook the worm under the collar and leave both ends to wiggle freely.

One good way to add weight to a worm rig for trout is to tie a three-inch monofilament dropper line about eighteen inches above the hook. Split-shot sinkers can be added to the dropper or removed as needed, without risk of damage to the casting line. If a sinker gets caught between a couple of rocks, it will usually slip off the end of the dropper. You don't risk a broken line or the loss of your hook and worm.

Anglers who fish the high lakes for golden trout like light spinning tackle and treble hooks baited with night crawlers. The trick is to place a plastic bubble about five feet above the hook and use a tiny split-shot sinker for weight. Small spinners and other lures are sometimes used, but the night crawlers seem to be more consistent. Worms are particularly good in the spring soon after ice-out in the lakes.

Crickets

The hatchery trout that survives the opening-day onslaught on the more crowded streams then gets a look at countless worms during the early weeks of the season. Sometimes your change to other natural baits will break a fishless spell.

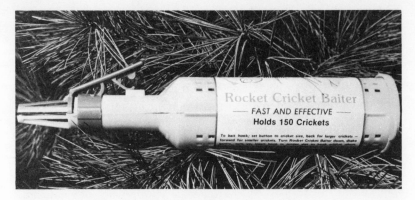

Crickets and grasshoppers are good natural baits at certain times. They are fairly easy to collect—but hard to control in a bait container. This handy gadget makes it easy by releasing one insect at a time.

"Those trout have seen a lot of worms," a Virginia game warden once told me. I'd been complaining about my lack of success. "One fellow," he said, "took his limit with crickets last week."

Crickets will take nearly all kinds of fish, and trout are no exception.

Gray crickets, reared commercially, are popular among anglers and available in many bait shops. Grays are common in the south, however, outside much of the better trout range.

But those black crickets that chirp through the summer and even invade the living room will also take trout. They're just as effective as the gray variety, but not as readily available. Black crickets are more difficult to collect than worms, but they can be found beneath rotting timbers, rocks, and other objects.

Crickets will survive a long time if provided with food and water and kept in a cool place. Sliced apples or potatoes will keep them well fed.

While just about any kind of container will hold worms, one for crickets must be more sophisticated. Crickets jump, and you have to take that trait into account. A container with a small opening that permits just one cricket at a time to escape is ideal. There are good plastic models on the market that do just that.

Crickets should be placed on the hook so as to look as natural as possible. They can be hooked under the collar, or the hook can be run through the body, as I'll describe later for minnows and crayfish. Running the hook through the body will likely kill the cricket, and this method should be used only when the bait will be cast and fished as you would an artificial lure.

Grasshoppers

Grasshoppers are much like crickets but—in my opinion—considerably less effective. Hoppers are abundant in late summer but nonexistent in early spring, the prime time to fish for trout with bait. Collecting a supply of grasshoppers is no problem when they're in season.

Grasshoppers are a reasonably effective summer bait, particularly in August. When the weather is hot, hoppers will take more trout than worms will in meadow creeks where the fish are accustomed to feeding on insects.

You can hook grasshoppers under the collar in the same manner as crickets, and they will stay alive and kicking. If they are to be fished deep, run the hook through the body and cast them as you would artificial lures.

Grasshoppers can also be fished on the surface with light spinning tackle, but the absence of casting weight will limit the length of your cast. If a hopper is to be fished deep, clamp a split-shot sinker four to six inches above the hook. The grasshopper can be drifted through likely water much as a worm is fished on spinning tackle.

Minnows

A natural trout bait that could receive more attention, wherever it's legal, is the minnow. Some truly big brown trout have been taken on live minnows. Live minnows often take the true lunkers of the trout world. All in all, a natural minnow is probably the deadliest lure for large trout.

"Trout usually start feeding on minnows when they reach approximately fourteen inches," Jack Hoffman, veteran Virginia fishery biologist, once told me. "But this development will vary between waters and species."

Minnows can be collected in small creeks and streams or in the shallows of lakes and rivers. A small minnow seine will serve well

While trolling live minnows on Big Cedar Lake out of Moosehead Lodge in western Quebec, the author took this pair of nice lake trout. Spinning tackle and eight-pound-test line proved satisfactory. The largest lake trout went ten pounds. Photo by Ginny Gooch

for this purpose, though regulations governing its use vary from state to state. Minnow traps are also good. Baited with bread crumbs and placed in a creek or shallow area of a lake or river, a minnow trap can be highly effective. Here, too, it is best to check the state regulations governing its use. Many bait-and-tackle shops and marinas stock live minnows, and this source is the best bet for the angler with limited time.

Other baitfish will also take trout. Good live bait for lake trout include four- to six-inch herrings, alewives, and suckers. The sucker is a particularly hardy bait. When trolled for lake trout, the live fish is used in conjunction with a series of spinners called cowbells or Christmas trees.

Live minnows can be hooked either through both lips or just behind the dorsal fin. I normally prefer the lips unless I am fishing straight down in a lake or deep hole in a river. Then the dorsal-fin hookup is better.

Even a dead minnow can be fished effectively on spinning tackle.

One way is to run the point of a long-shank hook into the mouth, out through a gill, and then back into the body near the tail. So secured, the minnow can be cast on light spinning tackle and worked seductively in a riffle or other fast water. A dead minnow, however, has considerably less appeal than a live one for most trout.

A weighted minnow harness for fishing deep is used in some waters, but I have had little experience with it and can't vouch for it.

Local anglers have their own pet rigs for fishing live minnows or other baitfish for trout. New Jersey anglers like to fish the Pepacton Reservoir with spinning tackle and six- to eight-pound-test monofilament. The usual rig is a one-eighth- or one-fourth-ounce egg sinker slid on the line and held in place by a small barrel swivel on the end of the line. Then a two-foot leader with a size 4 or 6 hook is tied to the other end of the barrel swivel. Most Pepacton anglers fish live sawbellies or alewives hooked either through both lips or through the back just behind the dorsal fin. The live bait is fished fifteen to twenty feet deep in May and June, and as deep as twenty-five or thirty-five feet in August and September. The fishing is usually best during midsummer months. Big brown trout in the five- to twelve-pound class are the fish most sought by Pepacton anglers.

Salmon Eggs

Salmon eggs are high on the list of baits widely used by trout fishermen. A few anglers collect their own eggs, but the great majority buy them preserved in small jars. Eggs come as singles or in clusters. The use of salmon eggs may be subject to state regulations also.

Salmon eggs are best fished on tiny gold hooks, just large enough to hold a couple of the little eggs. The eggs are lost easily, however, and it pays to check your rig frequently to make sure you're not wasting valuable time fishing with a bare hook.

The eggs can be stored in the jars in which they come. They can be kept from season to season, though they tend to fall apart rather easily by the second season. One way to toughen old eggs is to remove a day's supply from the jar and dry them in the sun for several hours. This treatment will probably harden them enough to stay on the hook.

Salmon eggs are most effective when fished without added weight and simply permitted to drift freely with the current. It's the same method that works so well with worms.

Some western anglers claim that a single salmon egg fished properly will take trout in the spring when nothing else will. They like size 12 shankless hooks, which are buried in the egg.

An egg is difficult to cast without losing it. You'll have your best luck if you flip-cast it or throw it softly instead of using a conventional snap-cast.

Those western anglers fish the salmon egg in fairly shallow, fast water, and they let it roll along the bottom—in and out of pockets and depressions.

Fresh roe baits are good for winter steelheads. The eggs are tied in small squares of red netting and fished on an eighteen-inch leader and a six- to eight-inch dropper, which holds the sinker. A three-eighth- to three-fourth-ounce split-shot sinker is heavy enough. Use a size 1/0 hook if the water is high and colored, but size 6 if it is low and clear. The dropper should be of lighter monofilament so it can be broken off if it snags, preventing the loss of the entire rig.

Other Natural Baits

Just about any insect that crawls or flies, and a wide variety of aquatic life, will take trout. Many, however, are difficult to collect, and some are so tiny they are difficult to fish effectively on all but the smallest hooks. Be sure to familiarize yourself with state regulations covering the taking of bait from fishing waters.

The hellgrammite is an effective trout bait, but it's more popular among bass fishermen. Hellgrammites are fairly easy to collect.

A wide variety of wet flies, nymphs, and streamers imitate just about every form of insect known to take trout. Most trout fishermen have artificial lures in their fly boxes or books that will do the job just as effectively as the real thing and don't have to be collected. If you must go beyond the more popular and readily available natural baits, you may be better off fishing artificials.

The scud, often called freshwater shrimp or sideswimmer, is a fine trout bait, one that many fly-tyers imitate. Scuds are most active after dark and can be collected with a small net.

The White River in Arkansas and Missouri, for instance, is alive with scuds. Rainbow trout feed heavily on them, particularly in the tailwaters. Scuds are also a source of food for trout in the spring creeks of south-central Pennsylvania.

Fishing Natural Baits

If a particular trout food is abundant in a stream or lake, you should probably give it a good try. The trout will be looking for it. Trout in large streams are more attuned to crayfish, minnows, and nymphs, but trout in brooks and creeks are likely to be more accustomed to feeding on land-based foods such as crickets, grasshoppers, and worms.

Meadows adjacent to high-country beaver ponds will yield natural baits such as grasshoppers, larvae, and worms. I once took a quick limit of brookies from a Colorado beaver pond on healthy earthworms I'd dug in a nearby meadow.

The size of the bait should determine the size of the hook. The bait should not dwarf the hook. If possible, position the hook so the point rides up. This arrangement reduces snagging.

The way a bait is rigged is important to how the trout sees it. Minnows are normally hooked through both lips when cast or trolled, and behind the dorsal fin for fishing straight down in the water or beneath a bobber. Dead minnows are often fished on double hooks and hooked so that they will ride between the two barbs. The point of a single hook can be run through the mouth, out a gill, and then back into the body (as described earlier), or into the mouth and out the anus.

Crayfish can be hooked in much the same manner as live minnows, but hooking them under the collar is also a good method.

The secret to the successful employment of natural baits is to present them to the trout in as natural a way as possible. I like the lightest tackle possible—thin line, a minimum of lead (or none), and a hook just large enough to do the job. Spinning favors this kind of tackle.

Natural baits are good early in the season when the water is cold, high, and roily. Use the current to bump worms and other baits along the bottom.

Many natural baits are more effective in streams than they are in ponds and lakes because stream currents give them a natural drift. This is the action the angler should seek.

Just recently I was fishing a swollen stream early in the season, and using worms—primarily because of the water's condition. The stream was crowded, making it difficult to fish artificial lures without disturbing my fellow anglers. I picked up a couple of trout, but then the action fell off. Like most of my fellow anglers, I was using split-shot sinkers to get my worm deep in the swollen stream.

Playing a hunch, I decided to remove the lead and let the current give my bait a natural drift. The worm alone provided sufficient casting weight for my ultralight tackle.

The change brought almost startling results. On two successive drifts, hardy trout smacked my worm. I managed to land one of them. Within minutes I had my six-trout limit, and I hadn't left the pool I was fishing in when I switched tactics.

An angler a few feet upstream watched in amazement, and I'm

not sure that he ever detected what I had done to change my luck.

When you fish natural baits on spinning tackle, by all means copy the dry-fly fisherman's approach of striving for as natural a drift as possible. This means eliminating the drag on the line and giving the bait maximum freedom to move with the current. For this reason, I rarely fish natural baits downstream. (One exception is a dead minnow behind a spinner. Then some resistance from the current may be needed to give the dead bait some action.) A downstream approach is also good for reaching inaccessible spots in a small stream; you can use the current to carry the bait into a likely spot.

I like to cast slightly upstream and across the current. This cast gives the lure a good deal of freedom, but at the same time I can maintain control of the bait and be ready for a strike.

Live minnows require different techniques. In deep quiet holes, let them swim freely. But in a lively stream, it is best to let them tumble with the current, emulating crippled minnows too weak to fight it.

As is true when you fish with worms or other natural baits, it is best to let the trout take the minnow and run with it. Too much resistance on the line may cause the wary trout to spit it out.

Lakes and ponds that have no appreciable current present different problems for the bait fisherman. But consider for a moment how insects and worms get into lakes and ponds.

Crickets, grasshoppers, and other insects fall from tree branches over the stream, err by leaping from a safe spot and landing on the water, or fall on the surface while in flight. There they kick and flutter until they reach the safety of the shore, drown, or are gulped down by a hungry trout.

Many worms are washed into the water during heavy rainfalls, or they get caught in the currents of feeder streams to eventually end up in a lake or pond. In fact, one of the best times to fish worms for trout is during or immediately after a storm, when the trout are alert for such choice food.

So the trick is to present the bait as nature would. This is not always easy, particularly when you are fishing insects.

Much of my trout-fishing experience in lakes and ponds has been with artificials, minnows, and worms. I find worms especially effective in fishing beaver ponds for brookies. I let the current from the main stream sweep the unweighted worm into the pond, or I cast the worm to feeding trout and let it sink slowly and naturally. Eventually, it will settle to the bottom if a trout does not take it. If I get no action within a few minutes, I retrieve and cast again.

Many anglers fish lakes by casting a weighted worm out from shore and working it slowly back in short jerks. This is a good way to catch rainbows.

Minnows, of course, are native to most lakes and ponds, but they live in the shallows, where there is moderate protection from predatory fish. Trout and other species enter the shallows frequently on feeding sprees, a good time to fish minnows. Trout will also hit minnows presented to them in their more usual hangouts.

Among the problems with minnows is their inclination to either dive for the bottom to hide in the weeds and mud or else to seek the surface and swim well above feeding trout. A reasonably heavy sinker will keep a minnow off the surface, and a bobber just large enough to prevent the minnow from pulling it under will keep it away from the bottom.

But this is not the only way to fish minnows in the quiet waters. Many more trout fishermen cast or troll them. If the water is not too deep, a minnow can be cast, using enough weight to keep it near the bottom, and then worked slowly back to the boat or shore. The sinker should be placed eighteen inches to two feet ahead of the hook so the minnow will swim off of the bottom. You depend upon the minnow—not the speed of your retrieve—to provide the action.

Minnows can also be trolled—again, slowly.

The best minnows are live ones, but a dead minnow, trolled or retrieved behind a spinner, is effective.

Bait definitely has a place in the plans of the complete trout fisherman, particularly if you're partial to spinning tackle.

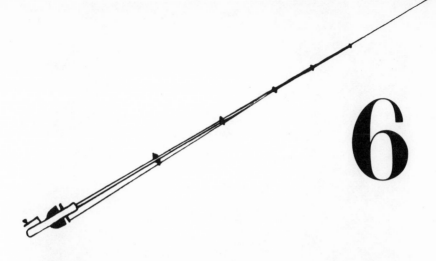

Other Baits

Between the natural baits (the worms, minnows, and insects) and the artificial lures are baits of another kind. In some ways, they're composites: natural in the sense that some trout consume them as they would worms or minnows, but artificial in that they're not a pure product of nature. In this category, we find artificial salmon eggs, cheese, marshmallows, and canned corn kernels (not a natural trout food).

Hatchery-reared rainbows are particularly vulnerable to these baits. The trout, fed on pellets in the hatchery tanks, are accustomed to such food. It is more familiar to them than natural baits.

I have trouble accepting this kind of bait. I either fish with natural baits or go all the way to the true artificials. But I must admit that at times I have resorted to the in-between baits in order to catch trout.

Many stocked trout streams are on private property and open through the generosity of the landowners. This rough-and-ready sign on a Pennsylvania stream was posted by a trout fisherman urging his fellow anglers to treat the stream and adjoining land with respect.

My experience on little Douthat Lake in Douthat State Park in Virginia is a good example.

This is a fee-fishing lake operated by the Virginia Commission of Game and Inland Fisheries. The tiny mountain lake is a jewel—clear and sparkling in a majestic mountain setting. Its cold waters, though infertile, hold trout well. Trout are stocked twice weekly, mostly rainbows, so there are always fish in the lake. You pay a modest daily fee, for which you can take a limit of five trout.

It sounds easy, but the fishing can be tough. Many anglers get skunked, and very few take their limits consistently. The lake is deep and has a narrow creek channel in its bed. The stocked fish go deep and are hard to find.

I have caught those trout on worms and on artificial lures. In fact, my largest rainbow to date came from Douthat Lake—a fine fish I caught by trolling a streamer on spinning tackle one sunny May day.

One summer day when I was having poor results there, a campground neighbor asked, "Why don't you try marshmallows?" The popular baits were available at the little tackle shop where you pay your daily fee. Usually, you have a choice of yellow or orange marshmallows, but I doubt that it makes much difference.

Somewhat reluctantly, I decided to give the marshmallows a try.

The bottom of Douthat Lake is covered with aquatic vegetation, and a bait of most kinds will sink to the bottom and disappear unless you take precautions. But those little marshmallows will float.

My approach to Douthat trout is to clamp a tiny split-shot sinker about eighteen inches above the short-shanked size 8 or 10 hook, sink the hook into the marshmallow and lower the rig to the bottom. The sinker settles in the weeds, but the buoyant marshmallow rides jauntily just above them. That is the only consistently effective method I have found for those Douthat Lake rainbows. Once you locate the trout this approach can be highly productive.

Marshmallows make good bait for trout in many lakes. A rig popular among anglers who fish the rich lakes of Washington employs a sliding sinker, a split ring, a twelve-inch leader, and a size 8

This youngster used corn to take a nice rainbow from a lake on the Jicarilla Apache Indian Reservation in New Mexico.

John Gooch with a pair of trout taken on spinning tackle and salmon eggs on Virginia's South River on opening day. Hatchery-reared trout will hit these eggs, cheese, and other such baits.

Many opening-day anglers use corn, salmon eggs, marshmallows, cheese, and other baits— successfully.

hook. The end of the line goes through the sliding sinker, and then you tie the split ring to the end of the line. Tie one end of the leader to the split ring. On the end of the leader go the hook and marsh-mallow. The line and leader vary in strength according to the size trout the lake might hold. Often a three-pound-test leader is suffi-ciently strong. The rig is fished on the bottom, but the marshmallow floats ten to twelve inches above bottom.

Many trout fishermen use kernels of canned corn. The corn is soft, is reasonably tough, and stays on the hook well. I have seen many trout taken on corn, but I have never used it, though at times I was tempted.

Many youthful anglers take trout on baits such as corn and cheese.

Apparently, the hatchery trout mistake the corn for the food pellets they have come to accept.

Cheese—ordinary rat cheese—cut in chunks will also take trout. It, too, no doubt resembles the food pellets doled out at mealtime in trout hatcheries across the country. I'm accustomed to fishing with worms on opening day, but I have had anglers outfish me two to one with their chunks of cheese.

Finally, there are the various salmon-egg imitations that are stocked in tackle-and-bait shops throughout trout-fishing country. They'll take trout, but some imitation eggs tend to fall apart and drop off the hook.

Most imitation baits are best fished on tiny gold hooks designed specifically for salmon eggs. The little hooks are good for imitation eggs as well—and also for cheese, corn, and marshmallows.

Trout normally gulp these baits down much as they do natural baits. These fish are usually hooked deep in the throat, and the tiny hooks hold well.

A major problem with most imitation baits is to keep them on the hook. They tend to break down in the water, so it pays to check your hook fairly often. Corn is probably the toughest of all imitations. (It imitates either salmon eggs, a natural food in some waters, or food pellets fed to trout in hatcheries.)

Spinning tackle is ideal for this kind of fishing because with it you can deliver a soft cast, one that won't tear the fragile bait from the hook.

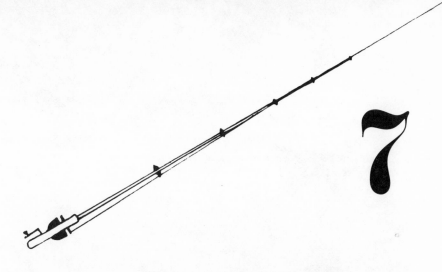

Trout-Fishing Basics

Originally, I planned to include this chapter's information later on in chapters on lake and stream fishing and in discussions of the different species of trout. But information of these kinds cannot be so neatly categorized. You need such know-how for fishing in lakes or streams and in trying for brookies or rainbows.

Trout can see, smell, and hear, and all three senses are strong. Authorities say trout can distinguish color and that they enjoy good vision in poor light and at night. They also have the ability to focus their vision on a far object and a near one simultaneously.

Trout do not hear voices. The surface of the water acts as a barrier, so a pair of anglers can talk all they want. Trout do sense vibrations, however, and those vibrations can be fatal to your chances. Water carries vibrations well. The successful angler will wade carefully, avoid noisy movements in the boat, and tread softly on the banks of stream or lake.

Trout do not hear human voices. The surface of the water acts as a barrier, so anglers can talk all they want to. Trout do sense vibrations, however, and anglers should avoid noises on the hull of the boat.

A trout possesses not only a fine sense of hearing but also a sensitive lateral line that picks up movement in the water. So bulky lures such as plugs and deer-hair flies are good for fishing at night.

Though trout can distinguish colors, they seldom show a preference. There are exceptions, of course. Red is often a good choice in lures during spawning season because trout feed on eggs. Also, colors that imitate a food the trout are feeding on should be the most productive. Brookies, cutthroats, and rainbows are more likely to hit bright colors than are brown trout.

The brown is the smartest of the trouts, followed by the rainbow, brook, and cutthroat in that order. This is a general ranking, however, and there will be exceptions. Some trout, like some people, are smarter and more seasoned than others.

Trout are almost always eager to hit in March, April, and May, but water conditions are unpredictable. If a large stream is absolutely unfishable, switch to a smaller one or even to a high-country lake or pond. It is a good idea to have those alternate waters in mind when planning a spring trout-fishing trip.

Fast streams can clear quickly. So if you find your favorite trout water too high and muddy, don't give up on it. Switch to other water and return in a day or so. It could be fishable by then.

Some trout anglers prefer the hot summer months when the crowds are gone. These anglers fish the pools early and late and the riffles at odd times. A good time to fish a summer stream is immediately after the water drops to its normal level following a storm. The cold rainwater invigorates the trout and starts them feeding.

Experienced anglers, if they can possibly do so, refrain from wading during the fall months. Streams then are low, and the water is extremely clear. This condition can also occur in lakes and ponds. Wise autumn anglers fish from the banks and use boulders, brush, trees, or anything else available to conceal their approach to the water.

Big trout do not always choose the deepest water for their hiding place, often lying in water only two to three feet deep. They like bottoms that provide camouflage, and they shun light sandy bottoms and light ledges as much as possible. Pools and long, deep flats often hold good trout. Trout avoid strong currents when resting, but they may move a good distance from their hideout to a feeding area in a pool.

Spoons can be good in the high country when trout refuse flies. Try spoons during the summer when the trout are deep, or in the spring when the water is muddy or roily and very cold. When the retrieve is interrupted, a spoon does not fall dead, as a jig does. The spoon flutters toward the bottom, and this can be a deadly moment. Even when trolling you can get a similar effect by dropping your rod tip or swinging it quickly toward the lure. Or you can sweep the lure toward the boat and then let it drop back—to sink temporarily.

A common mistake made by beginning trout fishermen is to use hooks too large for the job. A small supply of sizes 8 to 12 will cover most situations.

The plastic bubble designed to enable the spinning angler to fish dry flies can also be used with spinning tackle to keep wet flies off the bottom. Trout will sometimes hit flies suspended in the water more quickly than they will those rolling on the bottom.

By being persistent and casting to a trout repeatedly, you can sometimes tease a trout into hitting, even if it's not hungry. Apparently, it eventually hits from anger. And if a trout tends to ignore

Freshly stocked hatchery trout are a "breed" all their own, regardless of species. They are not accustomed to feeding on the bottom. Food pellets tossed to them in the hatchery never reach bottom before being gobbled up. Baits for these trout should be floated near the surface, rarely deeper than two feet.

your lure, try a different size lure. The *size* of the lure, rather than the color or pattern, may make the difference.

If a trout insists upon following your lure without hitting, try stopping the retrieve periodically so the lure will settle in the water. The trout may overshoot it but often will return to hit.

Freshly stocked hatchery trout are almost a breed of their own. They are not accustomed to feeding on the bottom. Why? Because the pellets they live on in the hatcheries seldom reach bottom before being gobbled up. Float your bait near the surface—rarely more than two feet deep—and retrieve it very slowly when a retrieve is necessary.

Look for hatchery trout in the inlets and outlets of lakes. A lake channel is good if it has a strong flow. In the streams, look for trout in the deep holes, near the feet of waterfalls, and around tunnels and culverts.

Artificial lures for hatchery trout should be small and brightly colored. Flyweight banana plugs and one-eighth-ounce spinners are good. Cut beef liver is an often overlooked bait that will take hatchery trout.

Brook trout tend to hole up beneath undercut banks, in deep, black holes or else in the thatches of drooping willows or other debris. The brookie awaits its food, so you must provide it. The fish expects its food to arrive a few inches off the bottom. Your ability to read the current is critical here.

If you get in a bind for brook-trout bait, try using the fin from another brookie, if this practice is legal in your state. The brook trout is not noted as a fish eater, however.

The brook trout is shy and sullen.

The brown trout is bullish, intelligent, and predatory.

The rainbow trout is flashy and often exhibits a devil-may-care attitude as it races into fast water such as rapids and riffles to snap up a bait or lure. The rainbow strikes hard, leaving little room for doubt, though hatchery trout are usually not so bold when first released.

The rainbow trout likes fast water and seldom takes a bait that's not moving. Here I'm talking about native fish, not freshly stocked hatchery fish. A rainbow can be persuaded to hit a bait or lure if you're persistent. It pays to work an area thoroughly—from different angles, using different casts and retrieves, switching lures and baits until you learn what the trout wants.

The high-country cutthroat is not necessarily smart, and its food is limited. The cutthroat feeds on a few kinds of organisms, which you should try to imitate. If you don't do this successfully, you may experience difficulty in creeling the brilliantly colored trout of the high places.

A brown trout may have a hideaway it uses for resting only. But when it decides to feed, it moves out to forage in the shallows, riffles, and other likely water for minnows and other food. When the browns are feeding, it is often possible to take several from the same area. But when they're not feeding, you should plan on covering a lot of water between strikes.

Because brown trout are extremely wary, it is best to make long casts. Thin lines and slender rods facilitate this tactic. If you can see the bottom, it is not likely you will get a strike from a brown trout, which can probably see you.

The harder a lake or stream is fished, the less likely a brown trout is to take a large lure. Tiny lures and spoons in the one-eighth- to one-sixteenth-ounce size are best on the hard-fished eastern waters, but sizes 4 and 5 wide-blade spinners and one-half-ounce wobblers may be a better choice for western streams.

During midday, you may be able to take browns by working your lure close to shore, where the fish are resting. But experienced brown-trout fishermen often wait until late afternoon, when shadows are long on the water. Then you can cast to the shadows made by boulders, trees, logs, and the banks of a stream or lake. Where it is legal, night fishing is good also; use Wulff flies in sizes 10 to 16.

These are just some of the trout-fishing basics you should know. One fascinating aspect of trout fishing is that innovative anglers are always coming up with something new. So keep your eyes and ears open.

Because brown trout are extremely wary, it is best to use a thin line and make long casts. Photo by Pat Gooch

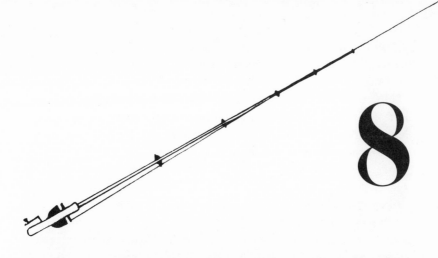

Fishing in Streams

When my thoughts turn toward trout waters, small streams are the first to come to mind. They're my favorite waters, and they're ideal for most spinning enthusiasts. The smaller the stream—provided it's large enough to hold trout—the more appealing I find it.

Tiny streams are usually remote, and many are tough to reach. They receive limited fishing pressure. One reason is the size of their trout: often the fish are not large enough to attract most anglers.

Anglers visiting another state are likely to fish the nationally known streams—the only ones they're aware of. Often some scouting will turn up little-known and seldom-fished waters that may provide much better fishing than the famous ones. Smaller, well-shaded streams are usually more productive during the hot summer months because the water is cooler than it is in some big streams.

Some steelhead anglers even seek out the smaller, less-known streams. These waters are less crowded, and the fishing can be better than it is on the better-known large rivers. The smaller streams clear quickly after a rain.

One of my favorite trout waters is tiny Ivy Branch high in the Blue Ridge Mountains of picturesque Shenandoah National Park. Native brookies fin those pristine waters, and a park limit of five eight-inchers can come quickly on a good day. Ideally, it is dry-fly water, but I find ultralight spinning tackle easier to pack in on the rugged hike to the stream. Even more important, the spinning tackle solves the problem of limited room for a back-cast.

The same kind of streams in the western mountains often hold cutthroat trout. In both instances, the water is likely to be extremely clear, and the thinnest line available should be used. Move as cautiously as possible. But if you spook a trout, take time to study the water and see where the fish was resting.

Pinpoint accuracy is necessary on such tiny streams, and you may

Jack Birckhead fishes the headwaters of Colorado's West Divide Creek for native rainbow trout. The rainbow is a native of the west.

need to move from one side of the stream to the other to cast a lure so it will drift into the right spot.

I like to work upstream on such waters, for several reasons. Since the water in the small streams is usually crystal clear and shallow, the trout are spooky. Cast your shadow on a good pool and you are through for at least fifteen minutes. Brookies and most other stream trout lie with their heads into the current. Their food approaches from that direction. Except for feeding time, though, they rarely lie in the open current unless the oxygen content of the stream is low. An angler approaching from the rear is less likely to spook the fish than one meeting them head-on from upstream.

The steep gradient of these mountain streams also favors an upstream approach. The angler moving from downstream presents a lower silhouette. Often a small waterfall will completely conceal your approach from the fish in the pool immediately above.

One exception I make to this upstream approach is when the sun,

On a wet day in May, the author fishes the headwaters of Virginia's Ivy Branch. Brook trout are native to these waters. Artificial flies only are permitted, but they can be fished on spinning tackle when weighted for casting.

low in early morning or late afternoon, casts my shadow on the water. Then adjustments must be made. A downstream approach may become temporarily necessary. Another exception comes when I am baitfishing which is rare. From upstream it is easier to drift a bait into a hard-to-reach spot. And when I wade downstream, I do stir up the bottom slightly—perhaps enough to cause drifting bottom life to prompt feeding by the trout.

Because these headwaters trout are rarely longer than twelve inches or heavier than one pound, the lightest tackle available is appropriate. A two-pound-test line is plenty strong, and it's inconspicuous to the fish. My favorite reel is a tiny open-face style such as the Orvis 50A or the Mitchell 308. My rod is a tiny five-foot, two-ounce Fenwick, and I would use an even lighter one if I had it.

Snaps and swivels are too heavy for the delicate line and light lures used in this kind of fishing. I tie my lures directly to the line. When I change lures, I break one off and tie on the next.

Light spinning tackle offers a good bit of leeway in the choice of lures. The smallest and lightest are best for ultralight tackle—and for small brookies. I usually raid my flybook for a good selection of wet flies and streamers before I head for such a stream. A tiny split-shot clamped lightly on my line six inches above the lure gives me sufficient casting weight. And, of course, there is the almost endless variety of spinners, spoons, tiny plugs, jigs, and other spinning lures that can be brought into play. But flies and streamers are so effective that I rarely use anything else in such circumstances.

While I rarely use natural baits on these little streams, they too are productive and convenient for fishing on light spinning tackle. Brook trout are particularly susceptible to well-presented worms. Use small ones, those dug from the garden in the spring, or red wigglers available at most bait shops.

Some anglers wade wet when fishing these tiny headwaters streams. They do not like to lug chest waders or hip boots on the long hike to the stream. Neither do I; but neither do I like wet feet. My solution is light stocking-foot waders that roll into a packet that will fit into my creel. I wear tennis shoes over them, often the same ones I wear on the hike in. When fishing is over, I dry the shoes as much as possible, slip into a pair of dry socks, and I'm set for the hike out. Ankle-height wading shoes are better than tennis shoes, as they don't collect gravel and sand.

And while red shirts add bright color for fishing snapshots, they also tend to scare the trout. Clothing of subdued colors is probably better.

The timing for such fishing is worthy of thought, though the little brookies will usually hit throughout the day. My preference is to hike in at midday and set up a light camp. Then I can enjoy both the late afternoon fishing and also the next day's early morning fishing. The fishing is prime when the trout move out of the deeper water into the riffles and shallows late in the day to feed, and camping on a singing trout stream in some remote valley is an unforgettable experience.

Reading a small stream is rarely difficult. My earliest angling efforts were with bent-pin tackle, hornyheads, and branch minnows in a small creek that meandered through the family farm in Virginia. I learned little about trout fishing in that stream; it held no trout. But I did learn about currents, rocks, curves in the stream, and deep pockets. That little meadow creek taught me to read a stream. Maybe that is why I have a decided preference for such little waters.

The current can tell the trout fisherman a good deal. It carries food to the fish, and the trick is to watch its route and learn the likely spots in which trout will be awaiting a handout. Such places include the protected water behind boulders or logs, the undercut banks where trout can rest in the shade away from the view of predators, and other obstacles that offer protection from the never-ending surge of the current.

Regardless of whether you're fishing with dry flies or wet ones, you should let the current carry your lure to the waiting trout. This is the way nature does it. Trout expect to get most of their food from the current.

The dry-fly fisherman who works upstream has no problem with the current, but the spinning angler must make some adjustments. In order to hook the trout, you must keep a tight line or the fish will spit out the fake before you know what's happening. Your best approach is to cast diagonally across the stream and let the current roll the lure downstream.

Using a boulder for concealment, the author works a likely pool in the headwaters of West Virginia's Williams River. Photo by Pat Gooch

This tactic can be difficult, for you must also conceal yourself from the trout in the clear water. So first you must study the water from a distance. Consider the current, the position of the sun, and the location of boulders, trees, or other objects that will conceal your approach. The spinning cast, done correctly, will put trout in your creel.

I rarely fish dry flies on spinning tackle, but the way to do it is to use a clear plastic float for casting weight. The float's hitting the water may or may not spook the trout, but it is a factor to be considered. Drop the float as lightly as possible, using the soft cast described previously for use with natural baits. The float should be cast where it will permit the dry fly to drift naturally with the current. If the float moves at a different pace from the fly, it may create drag that will give the fly an unnatural float.

The choice of fly patterns seems to make little difference, for both Coachman and Royal Coachman are good. Sometimes a tiny Black

Gnat will take more trout than most patterns, but usually I find that the native brookies like a fly with a bit of brown in it.

The key to success on these native brook-trout streams is a quiet and inconspicuous approach. Tread lightly. If necessary, get down on your knees to avoid casting a shadow on the water. Your shadow or the unnatural movement of a bush or tree limb can be fatal. You may put the trout down for at least fifteen minutes.

What I have said so far applies primarily to the native brook trout I know best in the east, south, and Canada. But the same tactics are equally appropriate in the west, where the introduced brookie now enjoys natural reproduction. And this approach will also take wild brown and rainbow trout that live in some of the cleaner, more remote eastern waters as well as throughout the west.

Recently, I introduced Harry Gillam of Richmond, Virginia, an angling friend who grew up and learned his trout fishing in Oregon, to fishing for the Blue Ridge brookies.

"I used to fish for cutthroats this way out west," he said.

My own cutthroat fishing has been limited to streams in Idaho, Wyoming, Alaska, and Canada, but I used spinning tackle success- fully in all of them.

As we drop downstream from the less accessible headwaters, we encounter put-and-take fishing, and more crowded conditions. Vegetation (which creates a back-cast problem on the headwaters stream) is less of a problem. But now you're more likely to have competition from other anglers.

The worst mistake you can make on hatchery trout is to assume they will be easy to catch. Except for the first thirty minutes or so of the new season, they're not that way. Even then, they're not always pushovers.

I have a successful approach to fishing for stocked trout, one I have used for years.

The put-and-take streams are crowded on opening days, but I don't object to this condition as some anglers do. Most opening-day trout fishermen are bank fishermen, and their mobility is limited. If you have chest waders or hip boots, you'll have little trouble getting away from the crowd. You can reach waters that the bank fisher- men cannot reach. Still, I always get to the stream thirty minutes before opening hour—to rig my tackle and select a pool for the first hour of fishing.

The Virginia daily creel limit is six trout, and I plan to take three or four fish during the opening-hour bonanza when the fish hit readily. Then I try for two or three others at a more leisurely pace as I move up or down the stream. Occasionally, I fill my limit within the first hour, only to regret that I must leave the stream and the fishing much too early.

Invariably on opening day I use spinning tackle—usually ultra-light. I also lean toward natural baits for the opener, since there is so little room to work artificial lures without snagging another angler's line or hooking someone on a back-cast.

In most put-and-take streams, rainbows make up the bulk of the hatchery trout, but there is usually a healthy mix of brooks and browns also. Most put-and-take anglers slant their tactics toward the rainbows but they also take a fair number of brooks and browns.

Because the waters of the average put-and-take stream are larger and flatter than those of headwaters streams, you can usually work as well downstream as up. Many spinning enthusiasts like to fish downstream because they get better action from lures retrieved against the current. This may be a questionable approach, which I'll discuss later.

Long casts are more feasible on put-and-take waters than on headwaters, except for opening day, when crowded streams just about limit the fishing to natural baits. When you can make long casts, you don't have to worry as much about your shadow.

The pools in put-and-take streams tend to be deeper and the water generally not as clear as in mountain streams. Except on opening day, you enjoy more freedom on a put-and-take stream.

Because the stream is larger, the trout have more water in which to hide, and they can be harder to locate. Additionally, the current of the larger stream can be a bit more difficult to read. Early in the spring when the water is usually high, the rocks, boulders, and other obstacles below which the trout hold for their food are more difficult to locate. Even felled trees and logs may be under the water.

Stocked trout tend to congregate in the larger pools. It pays for you to fish these areas thoroughly. If you're sure a pool holds trout,

The author and son-in-law Chuck McClaugherty set up spinning tackle to fish Stoney Creek in the Jefferson Forest.

keep at it, changing lures until you find something the trout will hit.

Browns, particularly, like the big holes, and even the native brook trout like to stay out of the fast water. Rainbows tend to roam a bit more. Though they spend much of their time in the pools, you may also find them in the riffles and fast water.

If the stream is not too large, the best bet is to cover just about all of the water.

Because the water early in the season tends to be high and often a bit colored, I will usually fish such put-and-take waters with natural baits, or with spinners, spoons, or spinner–fly combination lures. Later in the season, too much flash may startle the by-then-wary trout. Then I go to streamers or wet flies and use split-shot sinkers for casting weight.

In order to avoid a section of stream that's crowded with anglers, I may fish downstream when fishing put-and-take waters on opening day. I doubt that it makes much difference. The most effective cast is usually the one made diagonally across the stream. It can be made whether you're working upstream or down.

Usually, my most productive cast is the one that drops the lure near the far side of the stream and a bit upstream. Then as the lure tumbles downstream with the current, I keep a tight line, either by flipping the bail or holding the line in my left hand. I let the lure swing around until it's almost directly downstream from me. I work it slowly for a couple of feet, then reel it rapidly in for another cast. The magic moment often comes as the lure swings around near the end of the drift.

If I get no action, I may repeat the cast several times. But eventually I'll change lures, hoping to find something that interests the trout. It also pays to vary the length of the cast so that the drift will cover just about every foot or two of water. When the trout are not feeding actively it may be necessary to put the lure practically in their mouths.

The usual approach to fishing a stream of this size is to wade the shallower side and cast to the deeper water. On bends in the stream, the current churns out the deeper holes on the outside of the bend. So you should work from inside the curve.

The tail of a pool is usually much shallower than the top, where the fast water from a rapid or waterfall pours in. If you're fishing downstream, you may have to leave the stream just above such water and enter it downstream near the tail of the pool. When you fish upstream, you enter the tail of the pool first and don't have this problem. The tail should be fished first.

The larger boulders—even the midstream ones—usually protrude well above the surface of the water, so locating them is no problem. Trout like to lie in the quiet, protected water just below boulders and wait for the current to bring them food. This is a fine place to fish a spinning lure. But instead of casting directly to the spot, make your cast several feet upstream and let the current sweep it to the hotspot. Even hatchery-reared trout soon take up positions in such spots.

Large boulders may be obvious, but smaller ones that are hidden just beneath the surface are more difficult to spot. They hold trout also and are often just as productive as the big ones. Some hidden boulders may be just beneath the surface, others well below it. But they all shelter trout. The experienced trout angler has no trouble spotting these hidden boulders. The current often swirls noticeably over them. They are fairly easy to see in clear water. Polaroid glasses are a big help in reading such water and also for spotting trout deep in the stream.

On those elbow curves, you'll often find an undercut bank on the outside bend. Trout like to hold there—in the shade and away from predators. The current sweeps food beneath the bank for them. When you fish those undercut banks, you can have a problem getting the lure or bait positioned properly in the current for it to take the lure or bait to the right place. But don't get discouraged; some big trout are taken from such cover.

Other ideal hiding places for trout are fallen trees or collections of debris. But fishing them can be exasperating. When you get your lure or bait into the branches or brush where the trout are waiting, you're almost certain to get snagged eventually. One answer is to use thin-wire hooks. They will straighten without breaking and come free when pulled upon. This maneuver is best done by pointing your rod tip directly toward the lure or bait and pulling hard.

Another way to free a hook or lure sometimes is to reel your rod tip to within a couple of inches of the lure and then push the tip beyond the snagged hook or lure. You will likely free your lure, but probably you'll also frighten the trout. When you fish the fallen trees and collections of debris, you'll lose some hooks and lures in spite of all your precautions, but you'll also catch some trout.

The spots I've just described become obvious targets as you gain experience in stream fishing, but it pays to cover just about every bit of water in the average small stream: riffles, shallows, chutes, runs, holes, and pools. Even the rapids are good. Rainbows, particularly, like the fast water. During feeding periods, trout are likely to be found just about anywhere in a stream.

Most of the time trout will be found either near the surface or on the bottom, and the successful angler will determine this preference early.

When trout feed on top, dimpling the surface as they take food, they're easy to locate. It is a condition that favors the dry-fly fisherman, but the spinning angler should not despair. If necessary, you can use a plastic float and fish dry flies on your spinning tackle. I have enjoyed good fishing under such conditions by drifting worms just beneath the surface—particularly, early in the season. I have never tried the tactic during a May or June hatch, and I doubt that it would work then.

At dawn a few springs ago I was on a trout stream, experiencing only mediocre success but enjoying the spectacle of dawn's gray light fading into the brightness of a new day. I had been fishing red wigglers carried deep in the current by a small split-shot sinker. Then I noticed a trout dimpling the surface a few feet downstream. I reeled in and removed the sinker. The worm gave me sufficient casting weight on my ultralight tackle, and on my next cast a trout hit as the worm floated downstream a few inches below the surface. Fifteen minutes later I had my six-trout limit.

Most times, however, trout are on the bottom or close to it. Then you must get your bait or lure deep. This is rarely a problem. The average put-and-take stream, except for an occasional deep hole, is not very deep.

It is a mistake to use too much weight. The idea is to present the lure or bait as naturally as possible—to let it roll gently with the current. Too much weight takes your offering to the bottom, where it can get hung up between rocks or boulders. The trout may never see it.

Achieving the proper balance takes a bit of experimenting, and split-shot sinkers in various sizes are invaluable in this testing. Add or remove sinkers until your bait or lure rides just right.

A lure or bait that moves at the same speed as the current probably is a sign that the weight is insufficient. You'll feel no bounce along the bottom. On the other hand, a lure or bait is weighted too heavily if it bounces along the bottom at less than half the speed of the current and hangs up frequently. A correctly weighted lure or bait moves slightly slower than the current, and you feel frequent light taps as it brushes the tops of rocks, other obstacles, and occasionally the bottom.

Most spinning lures suitable for the rod, reel, and line you're using do not need additional casting weight, but flies and spinners will need to be weighted with split-shot. Again, you'll need to do some testing to achieve the proper balance.

Some Tips on Wading

Even the eastern put-and-take streams flow swiftly (particularly, early in the season) and the current can be surprisingly strong. Wading such a stream requires a bit of technique and skill if you want to avoid the embarrassment of a good dunking and the grief of a broken arm.

Caution is the key to safe wading—caution and moving slowly. Most anglers fall in their haste to reach either a favorite fishing spot or the other side of a stream. Hurrying is not only risky but also bad for the fishing.

A basic precaution practiced by experienced trout fishermen is to plant the forward foot firmly before lifting the rear one in preparation for another step. This strategy ensures good footing on a sandy bottom, or at least on a solid rock that is free of slime. Most tumbles occur when an angler moves one foot ahead and lifts the other one before the front foot is planted solidly. If your front foot happens to land on a slippery rock or a loose one, you're almost sure to lose your balance as you shift your weight.

Some anglers use a wading staff, which is a tremendous help in maintaining balance in a strong current. When not in use, it can be tied to your belt and allowed to float.

Though wading a trout stream can be hazardous, I've seen many veteran anglers in their seventies and a few in their eighties hip-deep in racing trout streams. They were thoroughly enjoying their favorite form of angling, and no doubt adding years to their lives.

"I take my time. Got plenty of it," one hale and hearty octogenarian told me.

Early in my own angling career, I got dunked on a couple of cold April days. Then I learned to pace myself, to slow down and enjoy the fishing. Though I now spend many days each year on trout streams throughout the country, I haven't fallen in years.

Which Trout Prefer Which Waters?

While brooks, browns, and rainbows, particularly hatchery-reared specimens, are often found in the same stream, each species has its preference in water.

The wild brook trout is very demanding of water quality. Even the hatchery brookie does best in the smaller streams where the water is cold and there is an abundance of quiet pools with soft, muddy bottoms. When you're in search of brook-trout fishing, look for this kind of stream—usually the higher-elevation waters.

The rainbow is less demanding of water quality, though it will not tolerate much pollution or the warmer waters preferred by fish such as bass and bluegill. The rainbow, however, is at home in the larger streams if the water is cold and clean, and the rainbow will accept water conditions that the brookie will not. The rainbow likes fast water and is as much at home in a series of racing rapids as it is in a cool, quiet pool.

The brown trout is the most tolerant of the three. It will do well in lower-elevation streams, the big ones preferred by rock bass and smallmouths. In fact, it is not unusual to find the brown trout and the smallmouth bass in the same water. The brown will accept warmer water than will the rainbow and is a bit more tolerant of pollution.

These are the trout—brooks, browns, and rainbows—found most often in eastern streams. And these species also support the bulk of the western stream fishing.

The western spinning angler can add the cutthroat, often found in small headwaters streams not far from snowmelt, and sometimes downstream in waters that may hold rainbows and other fish. The cutthroat is one of the more popular western trouts.

Other western stream trout include the Dolly Varden, the golden trout, and the steelhead, actually a rainbow that migrates to the ocean. The steelhead, however, is more a trout of the rivers than of the typical small-to-medium stream I'm considering here.

The stream-grown Dolly Varden is about the size of the average brookie of like environment. Stream fishermen can take Dolly Vardens through the summer, usually near the bottom. They hit the usual array of spinning lures—small plugs, spinners, streamers, and wobblers—and natural baits such as minnows. The Dolly Varden angler should fish deep in the holes, the pools, and the fast runs. The more productive water is similar to that favored by the brook trout.

The golden trout is found primarily in the cold, fast streams above timberline. These streams, though mostly swift, also contain stretches of quiet water.

Though steelhead fishing in the big rivers calls for special techniques (discussed in a later chapter), the steelhead in the smaller streams can be taken with much the same tackle, lures, and methods already described for the rainbow.

The arctic char is another stream fish that the angler may encounter occasionally in some of the smaller streams of the far north. But like the steelhead, it is basically a big-water fish and will be discussed later.

Locating the Trout

Locating trout in small streams is rarely the problem that it is in rivers and lakes. There is not a great quantity of water, and the trout is limited in its movements. The water is also usually shallow, and you have limited choices in how deep or shallow you will fish your lure or bait.

When I'm fishing small streams, I try to cover just about all of the water. Doing so is not difficult.

Some spots are familiar to experienced trout fishermen the world over: the undercut banks carved by the current, brushpiles, logs, deep holes surrounded by cover, holes between logs where the current may flow over the upstream one and beneath the lower one, eddies, and small whirlpools.

Brook trout, particularly, like to position themselves just outside fast water.

Look for any kind of water that provides the trout with protection from the current: slack water behind submerged boulders and rocks, deep holes at the foot of bars and riffles, eddies that turn behind rocks, and projections from the banks.

Midstream channels are likely trout holders. Choppy water in an otherwise smooth pool means swift water is overriding the slower water down in a channel.

Trout also like shaded water. Feeding trout may rest there to take advantage of concealment offered by the shade. Trees, high banks, and boulders all offer shade.

One way to locate trout in a stream is to stand well upstream from a promising pool and toss some insects into the current. If a trout rises and takes one of the insects, you can mark the spot and work that fish.

When you fish upstream, it's a good idea to work the tail of a pool first. When fishing a boulder, rock, or log that breaks the current, give attention to the pocket of still water just below the obstacle. Trout like to lie in the edges of anything that breaks the flow of current. Also fish both sides of the break. And don't forget the slick just above the rock or log. Big trout may wait there, resisting the current, and taking food from it before it drifts into the break.

Fishing Methods

Various methods for taking trout in small streams have been touched upon earlier. Above all, the successful angler will learn to use the current to his advantage and to avoid spooking the trout.

Before fishing a pool or any other stretch of water, stand back and study the water, the current, and the possible action of the trout. If the trout are rising, make your first cast to the fish nearest you so that a fighting trout will be less likely to disturb trout elsewhere in the pool.

When fishing upstream, as I usually do, I like to fish the water nearest me and gradually lengthen my casts until I have covered all the water I can reach without moving.

Some anglers like to get downstream of a feeding trout and cast directly above the fish so the bait or lure will drift by on a direct line between a point above the trout and the angler. Your offering should move by very close to the trout without spooking it. Some anglers insist this is the only way to fish natural baits upstream. If your cast is quartered too much, line drag may cause the bait to swing by too far from the fish.

When you're working downstream, one way to cover a good stretch of water—be it a pool, riffle, or shoal—is to start near the top and cast across the current. Work your lure slightly as it drifts with the current until the line eventually straightens out downstream. Make several casts from that position. Then move a few steps downstream and repeat the process, continuing in this manner until you've reached the downstream edge of the water.

A lure moving along the bottom will tap rocks, snags, and other obstacles, creating a sensation similar to the light strike of a trout. The experienced angler, when fishing this way, strikes at the slightest indication that the downstream movement of the lure has ceased. It *could* be a trout.

One unusual method of taking trout is known as dapping, a technique perfected by fly fishermen but adaptable to spinning. Dapping eliminates line drag. You use a short line and extend the tip of your rod over the water you want to fish. Drop the line straight down from the tip and move the rod at the same pace as the current. You need to know where the trout are lying, and you must be extremely cautious in your approach if you expect to get within a rod's length of a trout.

In the small, well-shaded streams, trout will hit just about all day. But early morning and late afternoon are the prime times there. Knowledgeable anglers often fish only from sundown to dark. This way they save their best efforts for the prime time at the end of the day. Too many anglers knock themselves out early in the day, then quit before the prime fishing time arrives.

You should use the weather to your advantage whenever possible. Cloudy, cool, and misty days are usually better than hot, dry, sunny ones, though these elements have less effect on the small, shaded streams than they do on larger ones.

Fishing on small streams can be good when you get frequent light rain showers during the day. You'll encounter few other anglers on a wet day. Under such weather conditions, pay particular attention to fishing the water near the bank. Try artificial cricket patterns, and remember natural baits such as crickets and worms.

Do not be discouraged by high, roily waters. Trout like to feed under such conditions—the high water is filled with food. But stay away from the main current. Concentrate on the eddies, pools, undercut banks, and quiet water behind boulders, rocks, and other obstructions. Good choices for this kind of water are small spoons, spinners, plugs; big streamers and bucktails; minnows; and worms.

I like to fish them downstream. The fish cannot see you in muddy water.

Choice of Lures

Probably 90 percent of stream anglers begin a fishing trip by tying on a favorite lure, one that they have caught trout on trip after trip. There's much to be said for such a choice. First, the lure is a proven one. Even more important, though, is that you have confidence in it. It gives you a psychological edge.

I'm convinced that this edge is important. If you think you're going to catch a trout, you're more likely to do so than the angler who has a negative attitude. But there is much more to selecting a bait or lure. The season, the weather, the waters should all be taken into consideration.

Check insects suspended in and drifting with the current. These are the foods most available to the trout, the easiest for them to feed on. You should try to match this insect with a lure from your selection. Also note how the current is handling the insect; then attempt to present the lure in a similar way.

One problem the small-stream angler may encounter is the eagerness of smaller trout. All trout will usually hit more eagerly in a small stream, but the little trout will often hit first, beating the larger trout to the lure. When this problem arises, try switching to larger lures, ones too big to interest the smaller, nuisance trout.

Every angler has a few tricks in the selection and use of lures. For example, a dead minnow permitted to flutter while held stationary in the current of a large, deep hole in a small stream will often attract big brook trout. And because rainbow trout like to feed in fast water, it's a good idea to use larger lures that can be more easily seen in the jumbled water.

Hatchery rainbows like flashy lures, and the rainbow is an ideal quarry for the spinning angler. Just about any spoon, wobbler, or spinner–fly combination lure will take rainbows. Fortunately, brooks and browns will also take these lures. Lures that imitate minnows and baitfish are the best choices for browns and rainbows, while plastic jigs are a better choice for the brookie.

Salmon roe cut into small clusters is a good bait for steelheads in small streams. It is illegal in some waters, however. Pink yarn can be used as an attractant.

The choice of lures for early season fishing is important. Wet flies such as the Coachman, Greenwell's Glory, Hare's Ear, Muddler Minnow, Muskrat, and Nymph are all good for the early season, and they can be fished effectively on spinning tackle. They should be weighted for easier casting and fishing deep.

Wooly Worms weighted and fished deep and slow in the current will take trout when the water and weather are cold in the early spring.

Spring runoffs fill the stream with food—worms, grubs, nymphs dislodged from the bottom by the current, and chubs and minnows. It is an ideal time to fish for trout with bait. Trout will be behind the big rocks, beneath the undercut banks, and in backwaters— backwaters that are high and dry during the summer months.

The cloudy or muddy water of the spring runoff is ideal for the bait fisherman. Trout cannot see you but they'll locate your bait by smell if it is placed near enough. The trout are usually near the bottom when such conditions prevail, and catching them is a combination of using sinkers of the proper weight, the right bait, reading the water correctly, and placing the bait at the right place.

Regardless of the season, bait can be successful in fishing a stream immediately after a heavy rainfall. Terrestrial insects are good then, and so are flies and lures that imitate them. The rain washes the insects into the stream, and that is what the trout will be feeding on.

Small streams were made for trout, or were trout made for small streams?

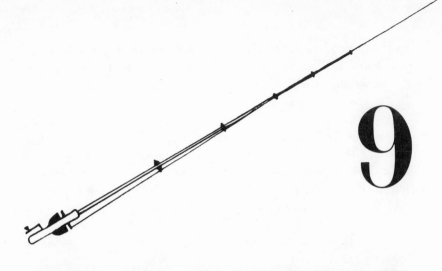

Fishing in Ponds

The trout fisherman who switches from stream to pond enters a new world, one devoid of currents, singing rapids, and the obvious signs that help in locating fish.

Gone is the play of the water, the swirling currents you rely upon for help in getting action from your spinning lures and baits. In a pond, you alone must give the lure the action needed to attract the fish.

Webster defines a pond as a body of water usually smaller than a lake—and that is what I have in mind. Beaver ponds prevail throughout most trout country, but there are also many tiny impoundments, artificial ponds in the high country, built for the express purpose of holding trout. Most are stocked by their owners. The Far North has millions of tiny potholes, natural bodies of water, but too small to be classified as lakes.

During my years on trout waters across North America, it has been my good fortune to sample pond fishing of a wide variety. Compared to stream fishing, I consider it tough. Trout fishermen generally agree that trout are harder to catch in ponds than they are in streams.

As we flew into a moose camp in Newfoundland a few years ago, my mouth watered. Below us were thousands of tiny bodies of water. The ponds had been scoured out during the Ice Age, and most of them held native brook trout. Later, with my moose hanging to cool on the game pole, I broke out my spinning tackle and took a fast limit of brilliantly colored brookies from the pond in front of camp.

"They'll go good for dinner tonight," said the camp cook as he took my catch.

There is probably no better pond fishing to be found anywhere than in those sparkling ponds in the maritime province of Newfoundland. Many of them rarely see an angler. Some ponds there have never been fished.

For the average trout fisherman, however, the beaver pond may provide the better opportunity. Some of the best brook-trout fishing in North America awaits the angler in such ponds, and they are found from coast to coast across the northern half of North America and in the high country of the southern United States.

Brook trout, particularly, like the quiet water and muddy bottoms of the beaver ponds. Several summers ago, I was fishing Cement Creek in Colorado's high country and having only modest success. There were brookies, browns, and rainbows in that racing mountain stream, which began at snowmelt. Near its headwaters an angler could find good cutthroat fishing.

"Why don't you try the beaver ponds?" suggested Gerry Reese, owner of the fishing camp my wife and I were staying at.

Most of those beaver ponds were loaded with scrappy brookies, and I filled my limit in a hurry. Though the brookies predominated, it was not unusual, I discovered later, to land a brown or a rainbow.

I soon learned that the fishing was much better in those beaver ponds than it was in the stream that fed them with its cold waters.

Beaver-pond fishing is generally best in spring and early summer, and again in the fall. Many beaver ponds are hard to locate and can be reached only by a long hike. Some are seldom fished.

Floating in a bubble, the author fishes a remote beaver pond. Photo by Ginny Gooch

Not to be overlooked are the thousands of artificial ponds built specifically for stocking with trout—usually rainbows. These little bodies of water dot the high country of the United States.

Most hold hatchery-reared rainbow trout, and many of them are operated commercially to provide fishing for tourists and rambling anglers. This is fee fishing on a commercial basis as opposed to the fee fishing that many state-fishery agencies have gone to on a limited basis.

Many anglers turn up their noses at such fishing, but a rainbow taken from a clear, cold, commercial pond can be just as scrappy on the hook and tasty on the table as one caught in the average put-and-take stream. I have enjoyed pond fishing for rainbow trout from the mist-covered Great Smoky Mountains of North Carolina to a high-country ranch on the western slope of the Rocky Mountains in Colorado.

These commercial ponds are also a fine place to start a budding angler's rich and rewarding angling career. As the saying goes, "Don't knock it if you haven't tried it."

In addition to the commercial ponds, there are thousands of tiny

ponds on public lands, and most are open to fishing. Sometimes you
pay a fee to fish. Almost to a pond these waters are stocked with
hatchery-reared trout as part of the state agency's annual stocking
schedule. They are all small waters, and many can be crowded on
opening day.

Now on to fishing those ponds.

Getting to the water is your first problem. Many ponds can be
fished from the shore—particularly those that are small and free of
bank vegetation. Many western ponds can be fished from the shore,
and so can most commercial ponds throughout the country. Most
pond owners expect their anglers to fish from the shore; such ponds
do not present much of a problem.

You do have a problem, however, when the pond is crowded with
vegetation and almost impossible to get to. And even if you can
reach the water, overhanging trees and brush may limit your cast-

*The author fishes a small pond near a public roadway in New Brunswick,
Canada. Chest waders are fine for such fishing if the water is not too deep.*
Photo by Ginny Gooch

A canvas-covered inflated tube is fine for fishing remote ponds where there are no boats and packing in a boat would be just about impossible. This "bubble" is light and easy to carry.

ing room. Here the spinning angler has a definite advantage over the fisherman with conventional flyfishing tackle. Such a pond must usually be either waded or fished from a boat.

Small ponds can be waded, but the water is often deep—even close to shore. Chest waders are recommended over hip boots. The bottoms of most ponds are soft and mucky, making wading tricky and uncomfortable. Some ponds are too deep to wade, even in chest waders. Then some other method must be used.

Small boats are ideal for tiny trout ponds, but they're seldom available. And if the pond is remote, getting a boat to it can be a problem.

Some anglers build rafts from dry logs on the shore. Others pack in folding boats that can be inflated on the shore.

Still another approach, one that I prefer, is the use of a canvas bubble, a cover into which is fitted an automobile inner tube. A harness provides a comfortable seat. These bubbles are light and easy to transport into remote, trout-rich ponds.

I have found pond trout, brookies particularly, even spookier than stream fish. This is especially so on a calm day without a breeze to ripple the water. The approach to pond trout should be just as stealthy as that to stream fish. This can be difficult when dense bank vegetation forces you into the water. Then your best move is to maintain a low profile and make long casts. Spinning makes such casts easy.

On a stream, the flow of the water will often break up your outline. This is particularly true near the head of a pool where the rapids churning into the hole keep a constant cover of bubbles and roostertails on the surface. Such water is rarely found in a pond except sometimes near the mouth of a fast feeder stream.

You must rely upon stealth, a low profile, and subdued clothing to keep from spooking your quarry.

The weather can be your ally. For example, a light rain that breaks up the surface of the pond makes it easier for you to conceal your approach. A light wind or breeze that keeps a ripple on the water will do the same thing.

The time of the day is also important. You'll be less conspicuous during the gray light of dawn or dusk than you will at midday in bright sunlight.

If you're successful in concealing your approach from the trout, you'll be a step ahead as you prepare to work the fertile waters of a beaver pond or some other tiny body of cold water.

Locating Pond Trout

Finding the trout in a pond can be tough because the usual stream signs (quiet water behind boulders, swirling water at the foot of rapids, undercut banks, and others) are not there.

But you can do better than just cast blindly to a spot of flat water. It's also true that you can cover the strange waters of a small pond quickly and thereby learn some of its secrets.

Feeder streams bring food to the fish. A beaver pond and many another small pond may have only one such stream. In fact, some glacier-carved ponds may have none. But where you find them, the mouths of such streams are usually pond hotspots. Trout like to gather there to await the food that drifts in on the current. It's a good spot to begin fishing a pond. But once you take a trout or two from such a spot, the remaining trout may have become frightened and refuse to hit. Then your only alternative is to move on and return later, after the trout have resumed their feeding stations. Then the inlet fishing can be just as good as it was initially. If there are several such streams, you can alternate among them.

All trout like cold water, and many ponds are fed by spring water bubbling up from the bottom of the pond. These springs are not always easy to pinpoint, particularly if the water is very deep. But once you spot one, it's almost a sure bet for trout. If you find trout congregated near the bottom in a certain part of a pond, it's almost certain that they're favoring the icy water of a bubbling spring. Sometimes a clear spot in a patch of aquatic growth on the bottom of a pond indicates a spring.

During hot or warm weather, beaver-pond trout tend to gather in the deepest water, usually, just behind the dam.

In the cold, clear waters of the high-country ponds and lakes, you can often spot trout at depths of five to ten feet or more.

In pond water everywhere, of course, you're likely to find such cover as brushpiles, rotting logs, boulders, and weed beds, all clues to trout hangouts. "Fish the *structure*," bass fishermen advise.

This advice is equally applicable to the trout angler. Such objects in water offer food and cover. Structure also provides larger trout a place to wait in ambush for some unsuspecting baitfish, frog, or other tidbit. The smart angler works these areas thoroughly.

Trout themselves may give away their whereabouts early in the morning and in late afternoon as they dimple the surface for tiny insects or leap for low-flying dragonflies or other insects. The angler on the water at these two prime times will have less trouble locating the trout.

A thermometer for measuring water temperatures is handy in pond fishing. With it, you can judge the depths at which the trout should be lying. Brook trout, for example, like water in the range of 55° to 60° F.

Fishing Methods

I feel the spinning angler has an advantage over the fly fisherman when it comes to fishing small ponds, except early and late in the day when the trout are dimpling the surface. Then the dry-fly angler has the advantage. Even so, ultralight spinning tackle is entirely adequate, and the thin two-pound-test monofilament is less conspicuous than a long fly line laid down on still waters. I even go with one-pound-test line when I know the fish I will catch are brookies that rarely exceed a pound or so.

The light line also permits you to make long casts with your light lures or natural baits. This is particularly important in pond fishing because it permits you to stay in the background, well back from the water. And because you don't have a problem with your back-cast, you can back up against shoreline trees and brush when wading. They offer you concealment.

I sometimes like to go to side-casts in extremely delicate situations because the lure lands on the water more lightly. Spinning tackle allows me to do this.

A major problem you face on a pond is getting the proper action from your lure. Lack of current practically eliminates natural drift, and there's no pressure against which to slowly work a spinning lure to provide action. You're fishing dead, quiet water, and you must provide the lure with action. Spinning tackle gives you an advantage. You have the necessary tools to work your lure quietly and inconspicuously.

When you don't know what the pond trout is likely to hit, it's a good idea to start with a lure that has good built-in action. The spinner-and-fly combination lures such as the Mepps and Shysters are good; so are the Panther/Martins. Worked slowly through the quiet water, they will revolve seductively. Spoons or wobblers are also good. Such a lure will wobble when retrieved and flutter when allowed to sink. Be alert for a strike when the lure flutters slowly toward the bottom of a small pond.

In clear water, the brilliant flash of a silver spinner or spoon may be too much. If such lures do not produce, try gold or darkly colored ones such as green or blue. And keep on changing lures until you find what the trout will hit.

Sometimes any action at all or any flash at all is too much. Then switch to bucktail or plastic jigs, streamers, or even wet flies. The flies or streamers can be weighted with split-shot or strip-lead sinkers for casting weight.

The play of the lure is important. Some days the trout will hit just about anything thrown into the water, regardless of how you work it. In fact, during those brief and infrequent times, the trout may strike the instant the lure hits the water. No retrieve is needed. Usually, though, the action you give the lure is just as important as your choice of lure. As a spinning angler with thin line, a flexible rod, and a reel that permits you to vary the speed of your retrieve, you're ideally equipped to impart seductive action to your lure.

Spinners rotate best when retrieved rather rapidly, and sometimes such a fast retrieve may be the answer. On the other hand, a lure with no built-in action (a wet fly, for example) looks very unnatural when retrieved rapidly and steadily.

In pond fishing, you'll generally enjoy better fishing if you work your lure erratically. Make it flutter and imitate a crippled minnow trying to reach cover. I like to make a reasonably long cast, one long enough to make my presence unimportant, and let the lure sink a few feet. Either a spinner or spoon should flutter gently as it sinks. A spoon is especially effective as it flutters slowly downward.

I'm ready for a strike the moment the lure begins to sink.

If nothing happens, I lift the rod tip sharply, reel in the slack line a bit and let the lure sink again. I repeat this type of action throughout the retrieve, but I vary the length of the forward spurts and also the depth to which I let the lure sink between spurts.

If this strategy doesn't work, I go to a steadier retrieve and vary the speed. Or I may try working the lure to the surface and then letting it sink to the bottom. It pays to experiment. Keep changing the action until you come up with what the trout want.

In many shallow ponds, the depth at which you fish your lure is of little importance. There is very little water, and the trout can usually spot the lure from a good distance. It is important, however, to determine the depth at which the trout are suspended and feeding. In most ponds most of the time, trout will be either near the surface or just a few inches off the bottom. They spend very little time between top and bottom. In fact, they spend most of the time near the bottom, feeding on the surface early in the morning and late in the afternoon only.

Vary the depth of your retrieve until you learn where the fish are hitting, and then concentrate at that depth. In the larger ponds, an electronic fish locator might be helpful.

To become a successful angler, you should constantly experiment, trying different lures, varying the speed of the retrieve, testing various depths, and changing lures—until you come up with a winning combination.

Maine anglers who do a lot of lake and pond fishing for trout like to troll near the shore early in the spring, especially near the mouths of feeder streams. Trolling is often more productive when a slight breeze ripples the water. Some Maine anglers use two rods, one for trolling and the other for casting to the shore as they move slowly along. Most states limit the number of rods you may fish with.

Rod Cochran, a New York State outdoor writer, favors an unusual rig for trolling lakes and ponds for big brook trout. He removes the hook from a small spoon and ties a six-inch leader in its place. Then he ties a tandem or double hook to the end of the leader and baits it with a worm. He works the rig close to the bottom—or at depths of ten to twenty feet.

Trolling can also work in the high-country ponds when a boat is available. Try trolling nymphs approximately sixty to seventy feet behind the boat and near the shore. Boating or wading anglers can often spot the trout in the clear waters of these high-country ponds. Then a nymph cast five to twenty-five feet ahead of a cruising trout may provoke a strike. The trout may hit as the nymph is slowly sinking, but if not, a twitch or two of the rod tip may provoke a good strike.

Trout anglers in Washington State like to fish their lakes and ponds with light spinning tackle and a plastic bubble for casting weight. They fill the bubble with one-eighth to one-fourth ounce of water. For fishing dry or wet flies or streamers, they attach to the bubble three- to four-foot leader of two- to four-pound-test monofilament.

Another good trick for lake or pond trout starts with casting a bucktail or streamer and letting it sink to the bottom. It is retrieved in short jerks with a quick turn of the reel handle moving it forward about six inches. Let the big fly sink between retrieves and the hair or feathers will quiver and breathe.

Lures and Baits

Often, a trout fisherman will begin working a pond by using such a popular spinner–fly combination lure as the Mepps or Roostertail. Such lures are the very heart of the spinning angler's tackle. Sometimes tiny plugs may be more effective, but I have rarely seen surface plugs take trout. Still, I do not hesitate to try them if nothing else will produce.

Size 0 and 1 Mepps spinners and flyrod-size Flatfish plugs are proven lures in many beaver ponds of the high country. But in the high, clear lakes of the west, lures and streamers that imitate minnows or baitfish rarely work. The reason is simple: there are few minnows or baitfish in such waters. The western high-country trout feed primarily on insects.

For these high-country ponds in the west, nymphs tied with dubbing or fur bodies are good. Try black, brown, cream, and gray, and use hooks in sizes from 8 to 12.

Frequently, the flash and flutter of a spoon, spinner, or even a brightly colored plug is too much for a wary trout. Then you should switch to wet flies or streamers. Clamp on a tiny split-shot sinker just ahead of the fly for casting weight. Vary the action of the fly or streamer also, just as you'd vary the action of a conventional spinning lure. Flies and small streamers weighted for casting can be fished on spinning tackle, but small spinners and spoons are often better. Some big trout are taken on spoons.

If artificial lures don't produce, natural baits may, and the spinning outfit is ideal for fishing such baits in small ponds. My first choice for pond trout is the lowly earthworm. It's about the right size for small trout hooks, and worms are usually easy to find.

On ultralight spinning tackle, the worm will provide enough casting weight so I can forgo the split-shot sinker. The unweighted worm will sink naturally, and this is the best way to fish worms. Simply cast to likely water and let the worm settle slowly to the bottom—if the trout give it time.

If that method doesn't work, try hopping the worm along the bottom. Jerk it upward and forward for a few inches, then let it settle to the bottom. Repeat this process throughout the retrieve.

Various insects such as crickets and grasshoppers can be fished in much the same way, though I prefer to have an insect rest temporarily on the surface before it begins to sink.

Small minnows are good in the larger ponds, particularly the ponds that hold browns and rainbows. The problem: how to keep a minnow from seeking the bottom and hiding in the grass or weeds. Casting and retrieving frequently will help keep a minnow in the open water, or you can suspend a minnow at the desired depth with a bobber. When you use a bobber, a small sinker may be needed to prevent the minnow from swimming to the surface. Denied the bottom of the pond, a minnow often swims to the surface.

If you have learned your trout fishing in streams, ponds can be a new challenge for you and a productive one.

Fishing in Rivers

Now I'll get into river fishing where I left off with stream trout. The difference between a river and a creek, branch, run, or other small streams is never absolutely clear. I have fished so-called creeks that are much larger than other streams called rivers. But generally there is this difference: a creek or other small stream rarely reaches appreciable size before it joins a major stream; a river, though it has tiny headwaters, retains its identity and gains substantial size before ending in the ocean, a bay, large lake, or larger river.

Webster defines a river as a natural stream of water of considerable volume. Volume is the key word for the trout fisherman. As an angler, I think of a river as a big body of water, much of which is too deep and too dangerous to wade. Minimally, a river requires chest waders, and even then there will be much water I cannot fish. Often, the current may be too strong for comfortable wading.

Generally, a river is best fished from a boat or a canoe, an approach I'll talk about in detail in Chapter 11.

A river presents a wide variety of the angling situations you encounter in small streams, ponds, and even lakes. Many of the techniques already described for stream fishing apply to much of the water in a river. Long stretches of calm, deep, lakelike water call for lake-fishing techniques.

In the faster stretches of river, the strong current carries food to the waiting trout. And they wait at the foot of rapids, behind midstream boulders, and beneath undercut banks. The big difference is that everything is more substantial—the current, the boulders, the banks, and the water itself.

The vastness of the water gives the trout plenty of places to roam or hide. Usually, the trout are spread more thinly in the big rivers. Finding them is difficult. Few small pools or runs confine them as in small streams. On a river, you must work for your trout—more than on a small stream.

But there is still the current to provide action for your lure or bait. The current will drift your lure or bait downstream to the trout behind the boulder or the one lying quietly beneath an undercut bank.

You can get the maximum action from your spinner, spoon, or wobbler as you work it against the strong current, or let the singing rapids dash it rapidly downstream to swing around in the pool below as your line straightens out.

Almost always there is richer natural food in a river than there is in a small mountain stream. In other words, the river offers the trout strong competition for your offerings.

Both the season and the time of day are more important in river fishing. A big river, once muddy or badly colored, clears more slowly. And a swollen river is more difficult to fish than is a small stream. Spring rains can upset your river plans and keep you off the water longer than they can on small streams.

Because there is so much deep water in a river, the trout are likely to spend most of the daylight hours there, making themselves harder to catch. So river fishing is usually best in early morning or late afternoon, when the trout move into the shallows to feed. Fishing can also be good at night in those states where it is legal.

For fishing the Williams River in West Virginia, the author chooses chest waders, because he can wade deeper water in them and thus his mobility is greater. Photo by Pat Gooch

Where possible, I like to wade a river, regardless of its size. And because spinning tackle enables me to make long casts, I can cover quite a bit of territory even though water shallow enough to wade may be limited.

By standing and walking in the water I'm more intimate with it and can read it better than from a boat or from shore.

For the sake of safety, you should carry a wading staff when fishing big rivers. You can buy one at a tackle shop or make your own. Even a broom handle will be a big help. Attach it to your belt with a line so that it will float freely when not in use. The wading staff provides amazing stability when the rushing current of a big river threatens to knock your feet from beneath you.

Sometimes, though, wading is just too risky. Wading the tail-waters of a big reservoir, for example, can be dangerous because of the sudden release of water through the dam. Besides, many of the best trout rivers are filled with rocks and boulders, and sudden drop-offs are a hazard. When these conditions confront you, your safest approach is to launch a boat or a canoe.

Locating the Trout

Because a river has so much water and the trout are widely scattered, it becomes even more important that you be able to recognize signs.

I usually try the more obvious cover first—boulders, undercut banks, and heads of pools where the water rushes in. The boulders mean quiet water; a trout can rest away from the constant pressure of heavy current. The quiet water on the lee side of a boulder is also a good place for a trout to wait in ambush for food to drift or swim by. Don't overlook the slick water just above a boulder, where the current splits to flow past it. Undercut banks give the trout protection from predators such as osprey and other birds, and the current brings the fish its food. Casts will have to be made extremely close to the banks here, and into the current—if possible, just above the point where it dives beneath the bank. The current also rolls food into the tops of pools.

If the usual cover does not produce, I try other possibilities: the mouth of a tiny tributary stream, a pile of debris, a sudden dropoff.

Occasionally, springs bubble up in the bottom of large rivers just as they do in ponds or lakes.

Cutthroat trout like to lie where two currents come together, and along the line between slow and fast water at the bend of a river.

Trout seek the colder water, and that flowing in from a tributary is almost always much cooler than the river itself, particularly during the hot summer months.

Trout like piles of debris for the same reasons they like boulders: protection from the current, and ambush spots in which to await food. I have taken many brookies as well as browns and rainbows from around old logs and piles of brush.

Dropoffs in the river bottom are usually at the edge of an underwater cliff or the lip of a big, flat boulder. Trout like these spots because they can rest a few feet down in the deep water and watch for baitfish that venture into the deep water from the shallows.

If you just cast blind in a large river, you'll waste a lot of time and effort. When you're fishing an unfamiliar river, you should concentrate your early efforts on the more obvious signs, switching to other water as you learn the river. Learning a stretch of river may take many days of fishing. Some anglers like simply to wait for a trout to rise and then cast to it. They attempt to determine its route and then cast ahead of it. Successive rises may indicate its route, and usually a trout will leap in the direction it is swimming for the simple reason that it is looking ahead for food and attacks in that direction.

Keep your eyes open for trout. Look for them in the river. Polaroid glasses will help you to see what's beneath the surface.

The Bullpasture River in Virginia is a top trout stream, and much of it is big water. I prefer to wade it when possible, and usually I wear chest waders. I was experiencing mediocre results on one of my first trips to the Bullpasture when I founded a bend and spotted an uprooted tree near the far bank. The river was calm there, and the water was deep, but that uprooted tree held my attention. "Good spot for a brookie," I told myself.

Cautiously, I waded into casting distance and tossed a tiny spoon into the debris, risking a hangup. The angler who shies away from possible hangups misses some of the best water in a river.

My tiny lure plopped onto the surface and began to sink slowly. I made a turn on the reel handle. The action had been slow that day, and I was unprepared for the sudden, sharp strike. But I hit back and wrestled a richly colored brookie from the snags.

I creeled that trout and cast quickly for another one. Again the response was immediate. But that temporarily was the end of the action.

I spent quite a while in that big hole that bright spring morning, and periodically I revisited the upturned tree. It yielded another pair of brookies before I finally gave up and moved on. Brook trout like quiet water and the protection of debris.

I know the Bullpasture better now, and over the years I have unraveled many of its mysteries. But that obvious sign, the up-rooted tree, gave me my start.

In the smaller rivers, stocked trout tend to congregate in the quieter holes, leaving them only at feeding time—usually early and late in the day. But some trout can be found in such water through-out the day.

Fishing the big holes in the river is a real challenge.

On a recent opening day, I fished the North Fork of the Shenan-doah River and was disappointed to see the trout concentrated mostly in one large hole surrounded by anglers. Most of the anglers, however, were fishing from the bank. So I slipped into my chest waders and quietly crossed the river to get away from the crowd. This is a point worth remembering. Most opening-day anglers fish from the banks, and the large rivers limit their mobility. The angler in chest waders can usually get away from the crowd in a big river.

Though some friends and I were on the river early that day, we found the trout in deep water, not in the riffles and shallows, as we expected rainbows to be.

I fished a green plastic jig that morning, casting it to the deep water, and I enjoyed good success in the big river. The trout were deep, but in open water. It was mostly a matter of raking the bottom for them. I covered a lot of water and developed a sore casting wrist, but I caught rainbows.

These two experiences represent extremes of big-river situations: in one, the usually shy brook trout hung close to the heavy cover of an uprooted tree; in the other, the more adventuresome rainbow roamed the open water of a deep hole.

Michigan steelhead like to lie in the big, deep holes during the middle of the day and move into the riffles to feed just before dark. The steelhead is simply a rainbow that is spawned in a stream but migrates to the Great Lakes. During the spawning season, however, some anglers like to fish the early morning hours.

Western anglers believe the really big trout tend to avoid the large, quiet holes because there is very little food in them. They also avoid: (1) fast water over a clean bottom because there is no place to take shelter; and (2) the shallow, slow-moving water near shore unless a hatch is on. Those big western trout seem to prefer heavy water over a rough bottom of boulders, logs, and rocks. Rainbows like to hold close to fast water, or under it, near the top of a big pool.

The mouths of the big rivers create special problems for the western steelhead anglers. Steelhead (rainbows that are spawned in streams and migrate to the sea) often refuse to hit on either side of a barrier in the mouth of a river. Some anglers even dig channels through the barrier to the surf. Trout moving through the channel are more likely to hit.

The season should be taken into consideration in fishing the rivers. The riffles and shallow pockets that hold trout in summer may well be barren of fish in early spring. Spring is the season to fish deep; deep backwater can be good in early spring. Trout tend to be gregarious in the spring, often bunching up in deep holes and pockets in the mainstream, where they can feed with the least effort. Like most fish, the trout has slower metabolism in the spring.

Fishing potholes in the spring means probing deep. It may be best to stand on the opposite side of the stream from the hole and make a long cast. Retrieve in short jerks with long pauses between jerks. If the lure is worked too rapidly, the trout—slowed by cold water—will not hit it.

A quiet pool beneath an overhanging boulder is a good spot for trout in the spring, and so is the slack water between two currents.

Arkansas River trout may attempt to spawn in February, and when they do so they like to congregate below the lips of any falls. There they will usually be found near the bottom.

The autumn angler will find trout crowding particular pools. Find these pools and you find the best fishing. Autumn brown trout like the depths of a pool and the slow water.

"Old man river, he just keeps rolling along" reflects keen observation on the part of a songwriter. A river *does* just keep rolling along; it never dies. There is always some current in a river, though sometimes it's almost imperceptible in those long, deep stretches of quiet water. The river angler should never forget this truth. In your search for trout, the current can prove invaluable to you.

Trout love currents, lying in them with their heads pointed upstream. Some trout follow the current to their spawning grounds. Others follow currents to the sea, eventually to return guided by the surge of cool, fresh water as it enters the briny ocean waters.

Rocks and boulders create buffer zones in the current, and trout lie ahead of, behind, and sometimes beneath them. Pockets created by obstructions such as logs, rocks, and deep depressions are especially good during the summer because the water swirling around them picks up life-giving oxygen. The fast water favors the angler because the trout has little time to look a lure over and so must make a quick decision.

When the big rivers become high and roily from heavy rains or melting snow, trout often leave them and seek the clearer tributaries. The trout apparently need "a breath of fresh air." They may ascend the tributary streams just far enough to reach clear water, lying near the dividing line between the clear and roily water. It's a good place to fish natural baits—if possible, those found in or near the stream.

Locating the trout is half the game, particularly so in a river.

Fishing Methods

While the current can help you locate the trout, the fact that it brings food to the trout is more important. So your best angling approach is to let the current give your bait or lure a natural drift. Sometimes the current may be too weak to do this, but it is something you should strive for.

Often bait caught up in the current is dead or dying, so you should mix some injured-minnow, frog, or other natural-bait action with your other presentations. The best way to do so is to cast diagonally across the stream and let your lure or bait drift with the current, fluttering it with the rod tip as it moves downstream.

Your ability to cover a lot of water quickly with spinning tackle is an advantage when you fish the rivers. But all of that water can prove fatal to success if you try to cover too much of it too quickly. You will simply fish too fast, and this may be the wrong approach. The most successful angler is usually the one who takes enough time.

The current tends to be strongest on one side of the river, particularly if the stream is a winding one, as the best trout rivers usually are. At a river bend, I like to position myself on the inside of the curve and cast to the stronger current on the far side. I usually make quartering casts upstream and give the lure or bait some action with my rod tip as it swings downstream.

As the lure swings around and gets almost downstream from you, the line will straighten out. Right then the action of the lure against the current will increase dramatically. This is a good time to expect a strike. The suddenly "alive" lure apparently resembles a minnow frantic in dangerous territory. A frightened minnow is often the first choice of a trout. At other times, trout are attracted to crippled, weak, or lazy minnows. Make the lure struggle with the current as you work it upstream. A lure retrieved against the current also tends to shoot toward the surface. This, too, is a prime time for a trout to hit.

Depending upon your orientation as you face across the river, the current will flow to either your right or left. If the river is flowing from your left to your right, you should make your cross-current cast at approximately ten o'clock. But if the flow is from your right to your left, the cast should be at about two o'clock. It may be necessary to vary this formula slightly, depending upon the speed of the current and the action you desire.

A lure rolling with the current is much like a lazy or crippled minnow too weak or lazy to fight the current. It kicks and flutters as it tumbles downstream and is more effective than one reeled rapidly

downstream with the current or upstream against it. Baitfish simply
do not race downstream in a strong current, nor do they often fight
it going upstream.

An across-stream cast followed by a looping retrieve that covers
the fanned-out gravel at the tail of a pool will take good brown
trout, as will a lure danced through the eddies and runs at the foot
of a bar.

If you have no luck with the conventional cross-stream cast followed by the drift in which the lure eventually swings around
downstream, try working the lure upstream in six-inch jerks.

Occasionally, the better approach may be to fish downstream.
It is the easiest way to get to hard-to-reach spots such as the water
beneath bridges, undercut banks, overhanging vegetation, and overhanging boulders.

Michigan steelhead anglers often fish the big rivers by anchoring
their boat just above a likely hole and letting a lure drift into the
hole. Once it reaches the head of the hole, they stop the lure and let
the current work it a minute or two. If nothing happens, they drop
it back another three or four feet and repeat the process until the
entire pool is covered. The Flatfish is a good lure in this situation. It
should bump bottom occasionally.

If you elect to work downstream and retrieve against the current,
you should retrieve your lure slowly, hold it steady occasionally,
and even let it drop back once in a while. The current will provide
most of the action, and the slow retrieve and occasional drop-back
will give the lure the appearance of a minnow trying to move
upstream, actually a rarity.

Often in fishing downstream, you make quartering casts, permitting the current to grab your lure as you retrieve it. Or you may cast
your lure into the current and then work it free for a change of
pace.

When you fish upstream with spinning tackle, you may have
trouble getting the proper action from your lure as you retrieve it
with the current. Usually, your best bet is to retrieve fast enough to
keep pace with the current, using the tip of your rod to jerk the lure
forward a few inches, letting it sink and flutter occasionally. This
technique can be effective at times.

And when you're fishing upstream, either wading or by boat, you

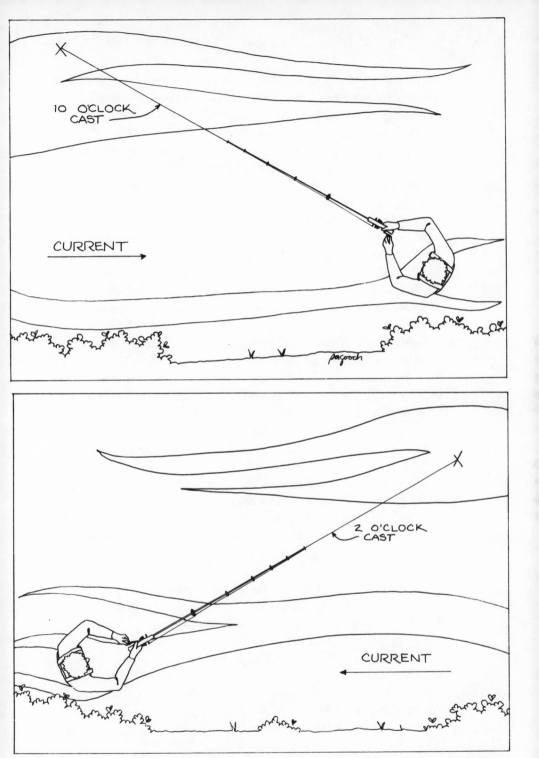

Depending upon your orientation as you face across the river, the current will be flow-ing to either your right or left. If the river is flowing to your right, you should make your cross-current cast at approximately ten o'clock. But if the flow is to your left, your cast should be at about two o'clock.

might be better off to alternate your position from one side of a river to the other and make quartering casts across the current.

So long as you make quartering casts across the current with your spinning tackle, it probably makes little difference whether you fish upstream or downstream in a river. On downstream casts, you can hold your lure in the current. On upstream casts, you enjoy some advantage on the jerk-and-flutter technique. In fishing upstream, you approach the trout from the rear, but this advantage is less important if you are fishing a big river.

Many springtime steelhead anglers like to wade and cast spinners upstream to spawning beds, where this custom is legal. Such fishing is usually best at dawn, but it can be good throughout the day. In the fall, however, they look for the trout in the tails of deep holes, and above and below boulders in water that is neither too slow nor too fast.

Fishing natural baits upstream can be highly effective in the big trout rivers. If the bait stops as it rolls downstream toward you, it's a good idea to assume you have a strike. Often it will turn out to be a hangup, but you can't afford to take a chance. It's a good idea to draw your line between the thumb and forefinger of your rod hand as you reel in the often-slack line. Otherwise it will not wind snugly on the spool. A tight line is helpful in detecting a strike but is hard to maintain in this kind of fishing.

When I fish rivers, I lean more toward natural baits than I do when I fish small streams. The river trout run larger—and wiser. They're more difficult to outwit. Natural baits give me an advantage, but learning to fish them properly is an absolute necessity. A dead minnow hanging lifeless beneath a bobber is not very effective.

I also prefer natural baits in the deeper waters common to rivers. I find it a bit easier to use the current to drift a worm or minnow deep into a dark hole. Spinning tackle permits me to cover plenty of water—a real advantage on a big river.

"Don't try to throw it too far," an old river fisherman once advised me.

A worm, minnow, or other bait will snap off on a hard cast. You're better off to let the current take your bait to the trout.

Before fishing a stretch of river, take time to study it. Notice the

An angler works a quiet pool of a West Virginia trout stream with spinning tackle. When fishing the big rivers, the wading angler should move cautiously, being sure the forward foot is firmly planted before lifting the rear one. Photo by Pat Gooch

deep water, the shallows, and the current. Try to figure out where
the trout are most likely to be holding. Then check the current to
determine where you should place the bait so it will be carried to
the trout.

There is no more effective way to take big-river trout than to use
the current to carry natural bait to them—to let the bait drift naturally. Let the current roll the bait along the bottom, using sinkers
if you must to get it down. When fishing a live minnow, use the
current to create the impression the minnow is injured and strug-
gling against it.

By positioning yourself upstream near a good current that flows
into a likely hole, you can make a short cast into the current and
leave the bail of your reel open so the line will peel slowly from the
reel as the bait moves with the current. By permitting the line to
slide between the thumb and forefinger of your rod hand, you can
easily detect a strike. Or you can simply watch the line, alert for a
twitch that will tell you a trout has your bait.

In fishing with bait, you rarely have any reason for the quick
strike so important in fishing artificial lures. The trout knows it has
the real thing. Give it some line, and let it mouth the bait. Usually,
the trout will swallow the tasty morsel and will be well hooked
when you take up slack and strike.

Sometimes when you're wading, you need to make long casts
with natural baits. For example, there may be too much deep water
between you and the current. To avoid losing the bait on a long
cast, it is best to make a wide-sweeping side-cast. Such a cast may
not look very attractive, but it is the safest way to deliver a natural
bait across a long distance.

Fishing on the bottom is not the best way to take rainbow trout.
Rainbows are inclined to look to the surface or the current for food.
However, bottom-bouncing (permitting a bait or lure to roll along
the bottom of a stream, hugging the rocks, gravel bars, and sand)
will take most stream trout. Use natural baits such as crayfish, hellgrammites, minnows, and worms when the water is high and roily;
use artificial lures when the water is clear. Slow-flowing runs two to
four feet deep are good. Also try riffles, rapids, tails of pools, eddies,
and heads of pools.

Steelhead fishermen like to bottom-bounce or drift fish, and when the bait stops bouncing, the bait has probably drifted into a hole or a depression. This could be a prime trout hangout. Get ready for a strike.

In fishing for river trout, you must learn to position yourself according to the type of water you're fishing.

When fishing an undercut bank on the near side of a stream you're wading, take a position a few feet above the hole that's under the bank. Cast upstream, but close to the bank. As the lure is about to enter the hole, slow the drift so the lure will swing around under the bank but toward midstream.

A small bank eddy on the near side of a stream is best fished by positioning yourself just above the head of the eddy. Cast along the bank, upstream of the eddy. Start to work the lure as it enters the eddy.

For a larger bank eddy on the same side of the stream, your position should be at the start of the eddy. Follow the general pattern shown in the accompanying drawing: make your first cast near the upstream edge of the large eddy, and make each successive cast a little farther downstream until you have covered all the fast water.

Your position for fishing a midstream boulder or other obstruction that breaks the surface should be almost directly across the stream from the bottom of the slack water created just upstream of the obstruction. From there you should cast to the top of the slack water and work your lure as it drifts toward the near side of the slack water.

If the boulder or other obstruction is submerged, take a position diagonally upstream from the spot in which you think trout will be awaiting food. Cast upstream of the spot and beyond it. Then begin working the lure as it enters the water you expect to hold trout.

The surging tailwaters below big reservoirs offer unusual trout-fishing opportunities. Understanding how trout react to the action of the water is important in fishing there.

The trout move with the rise and fall of the water as it is released through the dam. When the water is being released and the level is rising, the fish move about quite a bit—swimming into almost every part of the tailwaters. During the high-water period, which may last from six to twelve hours, the trout move to edges of the water or

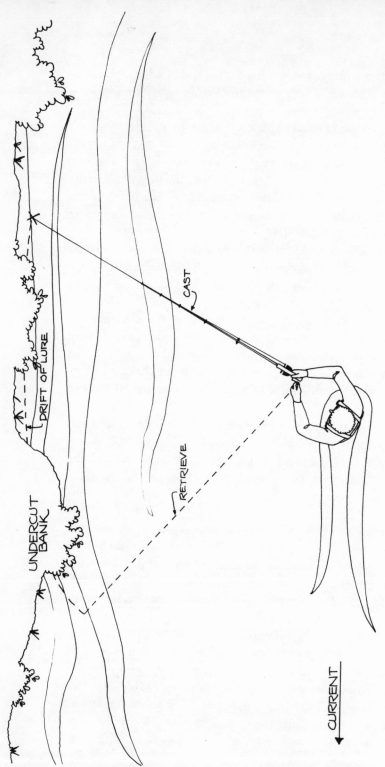

To fish an undercut bank on your side of the stream, take a position a few feet above the hole. Cast upstream but close to the bank. As the lure is about to enter the hole, slow its drift so it will swing around under the bank and toward midstream.

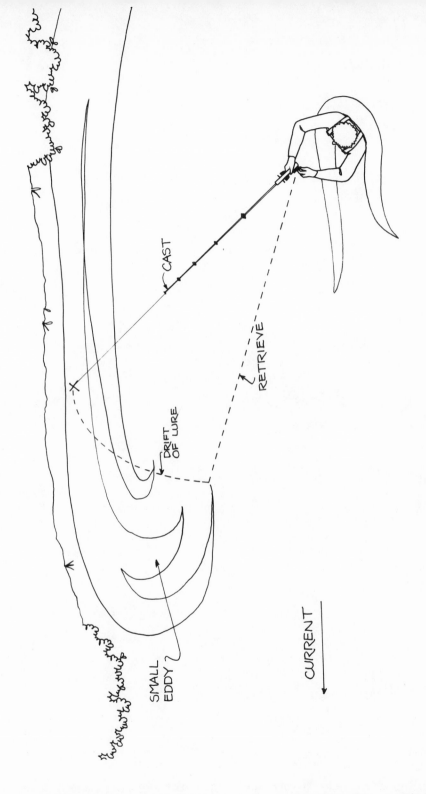

CAST

DRIFT OF LURE

RETRIEVE

SMALL EDDY

CURRENT

A small bank eddy on your side of the stream is best fished by positioning yourself just above the head of the eddy. Cast upstream of the eddy, along the bank. Start to work the lure as it enters the eddy.

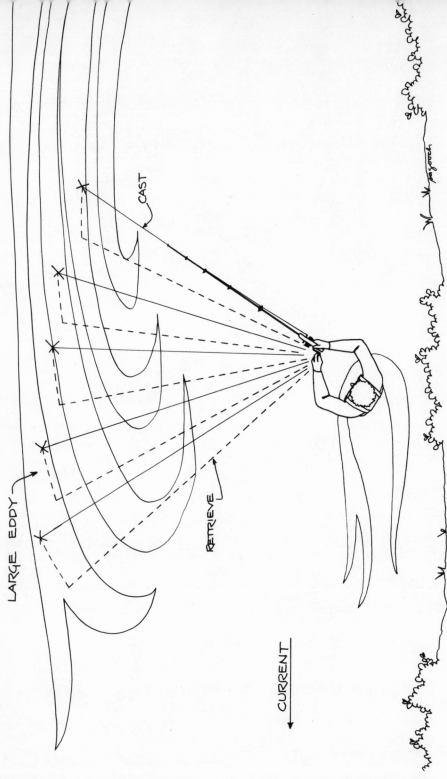

CAST

LARGE EDDY

RETRIEVE

CURRENT

For a large bank eddy on your side of the stream, position yourself at the start of the eddy. Make your first cast slightly upstream, and continue casting as the accompanying illustration shows, making each cast longer until you have covered all of the fast water.

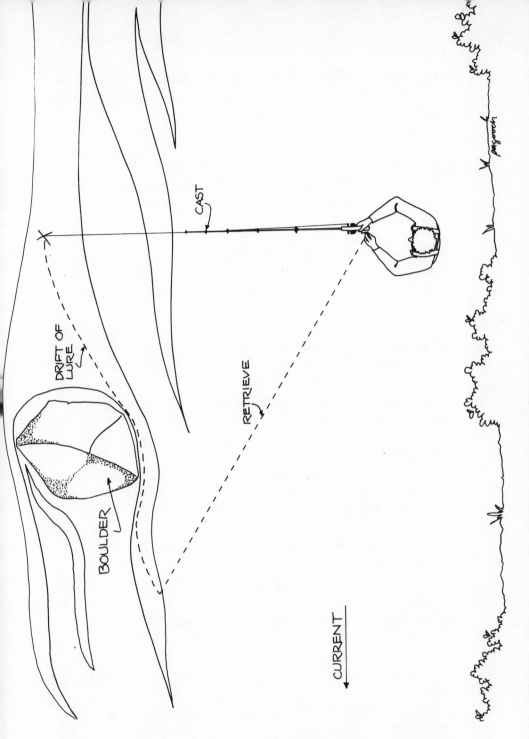

Your ideal position for fishing a midstream boulder or other obstruction that breaks the surface should be almost directly across the stream from the bottom of the slack water that's upstream of the obstruction. (This angler should ideally be slightly farther downstream.) Cast to the top of the slack water, and work your lure as it drifts toward the near side of the slack water.

hold deep in the main channel. The trout also range widely during the one to six hours it takes the water to fall. During the low-water period, trout will be in the pockets, pools, holes, and deeper rapids; around boulders, rocks, and logs; and under banks and ledges.

For fishing tailwaters during high water, you should use reasonably heavy tackle. But you can fish with lighter tackle during the low-water periods. Spoons, plugs, and weighted minnows are good for fishing the tailwaters; so are natural baits such as crayfish, minnows, and worms.

The tailwaters often give up trophy trout.

In the rivers, the largest trout take the choice feeding spots and often keep the smaller trout out. If you get no action from what appears to be fine water, probably a hard-to-catch lunker trout is holed up there.

Weather is important in river fishing, as on any trout water. The big rivers are good during a steady drizzle of rain. It is a good time to work those deep holes, and large streamers or live or dead minnows are effective. The big rivers also produce during a prolonged downpour. As the water begins to muddy, begin experimenting, changing lures frequently. The smaller lures may be good initially. But as the water becomes muddier, it is a good idea to switch to larger ones.

Wet weather is a good opportunity for you to avoid the crowds that gather on the more popular and more accessible rivers. You'll catch more fish and do so in near solitude.

Pacific steelhead anglers like to fish when the rivers begin to drop after a heavy rain. The trout hit best when the water is just beginning to become clear.

When those western steelhead streams are low and clear in the summer, wise anglers who can do so await cloudy, overcast days. A slight breeze that ripples the water is also helpful. Under such conditions, the fishing is usually best from around 9:00 A.M. to noon and again from late afternoon to late evening.

During low, clear water, the trout often congregate in the deeper holes. Fishing just at dusk can be good then.

Many truly big trout are taken during foul weather—and at night where fishing then is legal.

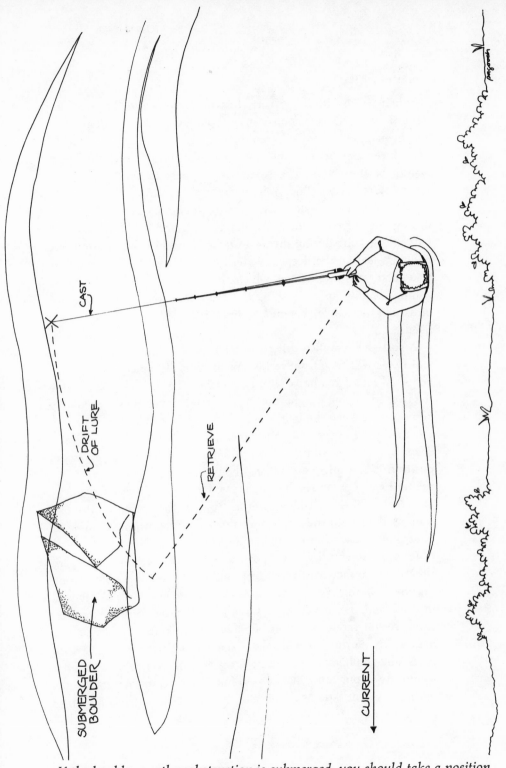

CAST

DRIFT OF LURE

RETRIEVE

SUBMERGED BOULDER

CURRENT

If the boulder or other obstruction is submerged, you should take a position diagonally upstream from the spot on which you think a trout will be awaiting food. You should cast upstream of the spot and beyond it, then begin working the lure as it enters the water expected to hold trout.

Lures and Bait

When fishing the big rivers, I lean toward larger lures, bigger natural baits, heavy spoons, larger spinner–fly combination lures, and even small plugs and crankbaits designed for spinning tackle. Such lures cast better, and it is easier for me to cover the larger waters of the rivers. The same lures appeal to the bigger trout you're more likely to find in the rivers.

Natural baits are good when you use spinning tackle on a river during the spring when the water is high and cold. And natural bait can be good during the heat of the summer when the trout are hanging deep in the deepest water the river has. Natural baits are also good for winter fishing, which may be nothing more than bank-fishing (baiting up and fishing the deep holes from the riverbank) or fishing from an anchored boat. Spinning tackle serves fine in such fishing.

A soft-shell crayfish drifted through pools, riffles, pockets, runs, and holes will take trout rather consistently. In quiet water, it can be fished on a plain hook with no weight. The crayfish will provide the needed casting weight, but in fast water a split-shot or two may be needed to keep the bait deep. In extremely fast water or rapids, you may need to use a bottom rig with a sinker to get the bait really deep. Rather than run the hook through the crayfish, some anglers position it beneath the crayfish's body and hold it in place with a rubber band. Of course, the crayfish will live longer that way.

A live killifish will take sea-run trout in the spring as the fish come and go with the tide. The fishing is usually best a couple of hours before and after the high and low tides.

Trout diets vary by river. For example, live crayfish fished very slowly on the bottom in the deep holes will take big trout during the winter in the White River of Arkansas. Some anglers like to peel the tail and use it for bait. On the Little Red River, however, crayfish will rarely produce, but lively worms are good. The sow bug, a tiny worm that will take a size 20 hook at the best, is also good, and the hook's eye can be threaded with very thin monofilament only—something like two- to four-pound test. The trout in the Spring River of Arkansas will also take crayfish, but live minnows are best.

The choices for use in fishing bigger waters tend to be larger artificial lures, bigger natural baits, heavy spoons, larger spinner-fly combination lures, and even small plugs and crankbaits designed for spinning tackle.

Those White River anglers like to fish the gravel bars where the water drops sharply, and the scud—or an imitation—is another favorite lure. Anglers there stand well back from the dropoff and cast a heavily weighted scud to the deep water and let it sink slowly. Split-shot make good sinkers. The scud is then worked slowly back and over the lip of the dropoff.

Michigan steelhead anglers like to fish with spawn sacks, particularly during the spring and fall. Spinning tackle is popular. Two-inch and three-inch squares of nylon stockings, each holding three to five salmon eggs toughened in boric acid, make good spawn sacks. They are fished on a drifting rig with a dropper to which split-shot sinkers are added or removed as the depth and speed of the current dictate. The rig is designed to move along the bottom. Anglers assume they have a strike when the sack stops, sinks, or changes direction. They hit immediately—hard.

Experienced cutthroat anglers use large spoons when the water is high and roily in the spring. "I like to get as much flash as possible in the torrent of muddy water," observed one veteran of many springs on the western trout streams.

Streamers can be fished effectively on spinning tackle, and they are particularly good in the fall when the water cools and the trout feed heavily for winter. One good way to fish a streamer then is to let it hang downstream in the current. Try guiding it into the quieter waters close to the main current, and let it sink slowly. Eventually, you will want to retrieve it if nothing happens. Do so in short darts of about six inches, with a slight pause between darts. A single turn of the reel handle is about right for each spurt.

Sea-run brooks, browns, and rainbows will hit weighted streamers, bucktails, spoons, spinners, jigs, and small plugs. Browns are especially easy to catch when they first enter tidal creeks, but they gain their characteristic wariness within a few days. Then they are best fished for at night, where night fishing is legal.

Weighted streamers such as the Jock Scott, Skunk, Parmacheene Belle, Royal Coachman, and Silver Doctor are good patterns in the big rivers of Michigan and elsewhere. Anglers look for steelheads on the spawning grounds and work toward the fish—often from upstream—to make quartering casts so the current will swing the lure toward the fish. The streamer is retrieved in short forward movements and permitted to drop back frequently.

Western steelhead anglers like to bounce a bait or a lure along the bottom such as the flame-colored Okie Drifter. They like to use an open-face spinning reel and six-pound-test line to get good casting distance. Normally, they use a dropper line and clamp on as much weight as is needed.

A spinner cast upstream and retrieved slowly down will travel close to the bottom. It can be deadly at times.

A wiggling lure or spinner is a good choice when fishing against the current. But when you're fishing with it, a jig—and sometimes a spoon—might be a better choice. Even when you fish *with* the current, you should maintain some tension on your line so you can detect a strike.

Big rivers are a real challenge to the trout fisherman, one that the spinning angler will learn to appreciate.

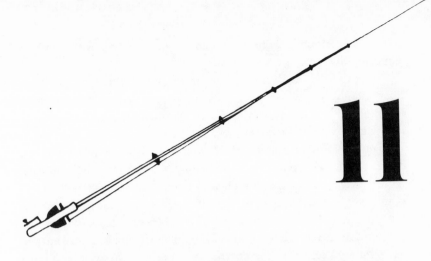

Float Fishing

Smallmouth-bass fishermen are generally credited with the introduction of float fishing to American angling. It's a fascinating way to fish: you drift slowly down a winding stream in a johnboat or canoe and cast to likely water. Float fishing combines a relaxed style of fishing with high adventure—particularly on a new river where you never know what awaits you around the next bend.

The method has long since been adopted by trout fishermen. It's the favorite approach of thousands of trout anglers, especially among those who fish the big western trout streams.

Spinning tackle was seemingly designed with the float fisherman in mind.

Float fishing is rarely a solo game. It almost always involves at least two anglers. In fact, a pair of anglers make a good float-fishing party. The usual required float-trip gear includes a boat or canoe

131

and two automobiles, one of which is equipped for cartopping or trailering the craft of your choice.

Plan carefully in deciding how much time will be required to float and effectively fish your chosen stretch of river. If you bite off too much river, you won't have time to give adequate attention to all the best water. The fishing will suffer.

After deciding on the length of your trip, drop off one car at the downstream exit point. Then both anglers load into the other car with tackle and boat or canoe and drive to the upstream put-in point. At the end of the trip, both of you board the downstream car for the drive back upstream for the other car. If both cars are equipped to carry a boat, you take your craft along upstream and don't have to return to the downstream point. Otherwise you must come back and pick up the boat.

Generally, the float-fishing anglers should alternate at the stern and bow seats in a boat or canoe. One handles the craft from the stern seat while the other gives his undivided attention to the fishing. When you're in the stern seat, you get some chances to fish on calm stretches of the river and assorted other times, but the boat should be your first consideration.

A canoe is fine for float fishing, as these two spinning anglers have found out. The motor will come in handy if they decide to run back upstream to float again through a particularly productive stretch.

A lone angler can enjoy a float-fishing trip, and I have often floated a good stretch of river by myself. If you plan a solo trip, though, you should be thoroughly familiar with the river. You should be positive that you can navigate all of the fast stretches without help. The boat you choose should be light enough for you to handle by yourself when you load it on your car or trailer at the end of the trip.

On a solo trip, you need help in the launch phase. My wife often helps me out. I drop my boat or canoe upstream and then meet Ginny downstream, where I leave one car. She then drives me in a second car back to my put-in point. My car awaits me downstream at the end of the trip. Of course, Ginny could meet me downstream at an appointed time, but this arrangement requires careful timing. Otherwise one of us could have a long wait. Floating a river does not lend itself to a tight schedule.

An advantage of float fishing is that it gets you away from the bridge areas, where the water is heavily fished. Some of the water you hit on a float trip is otherwise inaccessible and rarely fished.

Hip boots or waders can come in handy on a float trip. You may need to dislodge the boat from a boulder or sandbar, for example. There may also be shallow, productive water that you prefer to wade instead of fishing from the boat. *Caution:* Make sure your boat can't float away downstream while you're wading.

Usually, however, you'll be casting from a boat that's moving downstream, sometimes rapidly. So you should make your casts quartering downstream most of the time. Sometimes, of course, other casts will be desirable. A good example is when a fish strikes and misses and you want to try again, even though the boat has passed the point of the strike. So you make an upstream cast. Some anglers even mount a light outboard motor on their craft so they can run back upstream to fish a productive stretch of water a second time. Others drag a light anchor to slow their pace in good water, or even to hold in it awhile.

As a float fisherman, you invariably cast from a safe sitting position, so a little practice from that position is good preparation for a day on a river. Most anglers cast from the standing position when practicing in their backyard.

Western trout streams such as the Beaverhead, Big Hole, Green,

Float fishermen on the White River of Arkansas, a river long noted for its tailwaters trout fishing and its float fishing. Photo by Richard L. Gregory

These anglers are concentrated around one good pool that is easily accessible from the highway. They would enjoy better luck and more solitude if they could spread out along the stream. Floating the river by canoe or johnboat would permit them to do so. Photo by Pat Gooch

Lower Madison, Snake, Upper Missouri, and Yellowstone are all popular among float fishermen. These streams are usually unfishable during the snow runoff, however, and even dangerous to put a boat on. Good trout streams large enough to float-fish are less common in the east.

Long casts are rarely necessary when you're float fishing, but accuracy is important. You may get only one chance as the boat moves rapidly with the current. Casts should be made as close as possible to those likely trout hangouts—boulders, currents, and undercut banks. Float fishing calls for flexibility in casting. You'll make many short ones, occasional long ones, casts across the current, casts with the current, casts against it, and casts at every conceivable angle. Spinning tackle favors this demand.

Float fishing is a page well worth stealing from the book of the smallmouth-bass fisherman.

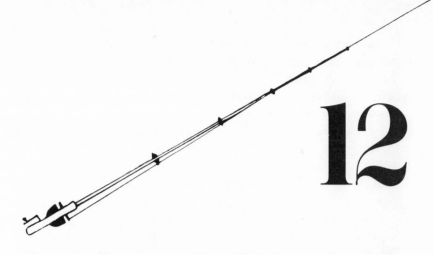

Fishing on Lakes

Just about any experienced trout fisherman will tell you that trout in lakes and reservoirs are harder to catch than those in streams. Locating the trout is the big problem. It's even tougher than the situation faced by the river fisherman, who usually has a few signs to rely upon.

Several things about fishing for trout in lakes make it different from fishing the average small stream or shallow pond. In a lake, the trout's natural curiosity is more likely to assert itself. In fact, the usual trout shyness so evident in shallow water may almost disappear. Trout in lakes are also likely to follow small schools of baitfish such as smelt and shad.

Trout like to cruise a shoreline, particularly during the spring, and many anglers catch good fish by working the shorelines. That's likely to be a novice's approach to lake fishing, and it's not a bad one.

"Cast a night crawler out there, and work it slowly back in short jerks," a fellow angler told me as I prepared to fish a trout lake on the Upper Peninsula of Michigan. We were standing on a sandy beach. His advice was good, though I didn't get the impression he was a veteran trout fisherman.

The big lakes produce an amazing amount of trout fishing in the United States, and not all of it is lake-trout fishing. Big rainbows, lunker browns, cutthroats, steelheads, rainbows that move down from the rivers, Kamloops, golden trout, Sunapee trout, Dolly Vardens, and arctic chars all are represented in lakes.

Some of the lakes that hold trout are enormous. The Great Lakes, for instance, produce lakers, steelheads, browns, and rainbows. Other examples are the Finger Lakes of New York State and many of the huge two-story reservoirs, where rainbows live mostly beneath the thermocline.

Trout grow to trophy size in lakes, and brook trout of two to six pounds are not uncommon in many western lakes.

One advantage of spinning tackle on a larger lake is the leeway it gives you to cover more water. But this freedom can be a trap. If you attempt to cover too much water too quickly, you'll hurry your casts and tend to work your lure rapidly. A slowly retrieved lure might be more productive.

Locating the Trout

Anglers who consistently take trout in the lakes are those who know the lake well. Most have learned the lakes by experience, perhaps almost by stumbling into productive water. They have the foresight to pinpoint such hotspots for future trips by lining up reference points on the shore.

The ideal way to pinpoint a good spot in a lake is to select easily identifiable objects on the shore so that lines of sight through them intersect at the hotspot. If four such objects are not available, take a sighting through two and note the distance of the hotspot from the nearest shore.

An unguided angler needs at least a couple of days to learn something about a lake—to find the deep holes, the inlets, and the outlets.

Most experienced lake fishermen, regardless of the kind of fish they seek, first buy a topographical map of the lake. Such a map or chart shows the contour of the bottom of the lake, the shelves, the dropoffs, the deep holes, the shoals, and other terrain features so vital to the success of a lake-fishing trip.

And, of course, there is the electronic "fish finder," or depth sounder, that serves the dual purpose of spotting schools of fish you pass over and also showing sudden changes in depth that indicate dropoffs. Such a device is worth the investment if you're a serious fisherman.

Equipped with a topographical map and depth finder, you'll have little trouble reading a lake. Consequently, you're a better fisherman.

While the stream fisherman searches for trout on a more or less horizontal plane, often in water only two to three feet deep, the lake angler must search vertically. Feeding trout are usually in two to ten feet of water in a lake, but they may be much deeper.

Certain other considerations are important in locating trout in a lake. Watch for natural signs that point to possible hotspots.

One such area is where a feeder stream enters a lake. The mouth of a small stream can be better than that of a large one. The water

Successful trout fishing in lakes calls for an ability to locate the fish. This major hurdle befuddles most anglers.

is usually colder in a small stream than it is in a large one and thus more attractive to trout. Baitfish may be more abundant in a small stream. The mouth of such a stream is an ideal place to fish small spoons or other lures that resemble tiny fish.

In the large lakes, even in most of the deep reservoirs, there are shallows that trout seek during the colder spring and fall months. These areas hold food (minnows and other tidbits), and the trout visit the shallows to feed. Most often the shallows are near the shore, but not always. Sometimes they are way out in the lake. In a reservoir, shallows may be over the top of a submerged hill, a real haven for baitfish.

These shallow areas will show up on a topographic map, and a depth finder will indicate them. During the summer, however, the shallows are rarely productive except in the more northern lakes or those at high elevations.

Determining the depth at which the trout are feeding in a lake or reservoir is a major angling problem. If you don't have a modern fish finder, your best approach is to let your lure sink slowly. As it sinks, count the seconds. When a trout hits, remember the count. Use it as a guide on future casts.

Most fish, including trout, seem to like boulder-studded shore-lines. Working such water thoroughly may prove productive. During a recent spring season, Walt Skidmore and I were fishing cold Summersville Lake in West Virginia. We were there primarily for smallmouth bass, but we found one rocky cove that held a number of rainbow trout, which hit our small bass plugs with vigor. The trout had been stocked a few weeks earlier and seemed to like the rocky cove. Also don't overlook the ledges and the lips of dropoffs.

Bridge abutments and concrete dams are always worth a try. The submerged concrete attracts various forms of aquatic life, which appeal to baitfish and possibly to trout. The trout probably feed on both the aquatic insects and the baitfish. Such places are always worth checking when you fish a lake.

Old docks offer food and shade from the sun. All kinds of fish frequent such cover. Give the old docks some attention.

During summer, trout in the big southern reservoirs tend to congregate in the deepest water, often that near the dam. They're hard

Luther Turpin fishes for rainbow trout in Cheoah Lake on the
Tennessee River in western North Carolina.

to find, but some anglers (often at night) take them from such waters.

Big browns and rainbows can be taken as a lake begins to freeze over. Look for those patches of water that rarely freeze completely. The combination of current and warm water attracts trout that would otherwise be deep in the lake then. Such water can be found at the warm-water outlets on the lake and near the power plants, mills, and other industries that rely upon the lake for cooling water from their plants. Man-made structures in the water often attract trout. Sometimes such places can be fished from shore, but you may find them fenced off. Then the only approach is from the lake by boat.

Casting along the sides of the current as it rushes into the lake from the plant can be effective. Just about any kind of spinning lure will work.

The brown-trout fishing is sometimes good along the south shore of Lake Ontario in the spring when the fish move into the warm-water-discharge areas to spawn. They are easy to locate and can be spotted rolling and jumping in the bays and inlets. Later, they go back to the deeper waters of the lake, returning to the shallows in the fall. This is typical brown-trout behavior in the big lakes.

The tributaries of lakes can be good right after a hard rain when the water is roily and loaded with food. The trout know this and concentrate near the mouths of the streams.

Lake trout can be difficult to locate, but a good place to look for them is around jumbles of rocks and boulders. You can expect to lose some lures. The lakers also venture into the shallows in the fall just before freeze-up, but they seldom move as close to shore as they do in the spring.

Don't spend all your time on a single lake if it's not producing. Try another one. Most lakes go through good and bad cycles.

Boats, Bridges, and Waders

The choice of a boat is important if you plan to fish lakes for trout. The variety you can choose from may be frustrating. The size of the lake has a lot to do with your choice.

A canoe is entirely satisfactory for fishing small lakes and even the shorelines of larger ones. But a canoe shouldn't be taken far offshore on big water. Flat-bottom johnboats are also satisfactory close to shore and in calm water. Whatever craft you use, recognize its limitations.

A fishing boat should ideally be equipped with two live boxes: one for the catch and one for the bait. It should also have an anchor fitted on a pulley so it can be lowered or raised quietly without ever having a hook-snagging pile of wet line in the bottom of the boat.

Many modern fishing boats have swivel seats that provide good support for your back and considerable mobility for you to swing around and cast to productive water or fight a trout that might switch from one side of the boat to the other. If a boat does not have such seats, portable ones can be bought for ten to twenty dollars each. They will fit most permanent boat seats.

The modern bass boat is a marvelous fishing machine that sees duty for many kinds of fishing other than bass. The flat deck and high swivel seats make casting to a shoreline a real pleasure.

Trout anglers can put a bass boat to good use. A most attractive

A canoe makes a good craft for fishing a lake, provided you use it close to shore or in protected waters, as these Maine anglers are doing.

feature is the electric auxiliary trolling motor often mounted on the bow. If you're in the front seat, you can work it with your foot, leaving both hands free to fish. I can think of no more useful tool for the trout fisherman who wants to fish the shoreline of a lake with spinning tackle. A bow-mounted electric trolling motor can be attached to just about any kind of a boat, and it's a good investment.

In addition to seeking these primary features in a boat to be used for lake fishing for trout, be sure you have life preservers, lights for night fishing and traveling at night, and oars for emergency use.

I have one objection to many bass boats—too much power. A ten- to fifteen-horsepower gasoline motor is sufficient as the primary engine for most boats, and too much for some. Ten to fifteen horsepower will move you quickly about a lake and enable you to make a quick run for cover if a sudden storm threatens.

Every tourist season, thousands of novice anglers take cutthroats from the famous fishing bridge over Yellowstone Lake in Yellowstone National Park. In fact, bridges in a wide variety of places afford opportunities to fish for trout in lakes. Most of this fishing is with bait because your limited mobility doesn't permit much casting. Jigging can sometimes produce under such circumstances. You simply lower your jig or doll fly straight down until it touches bottom, raise it a few inches, and then work it up and down in jerks. This, incidentally, is also an effective way to fish deep water from a boat.

Other trout anglers simply fish from the shore of lakes and also take trout. They too are mostly bait fishermen, but they possess an amazing amount of patience, an invaluable quality in any kind of angling. Many of them are retired people, and it's a healthy way for them to spend time. From hours of experience, they learn where the trout are most likely to hit, on what, and when. Spinning tackle favors their approach to fishing.

Some anglers simply walk the shores of lakes, casting directly into the lake or parallel to the shoreline. This approach is often used on remote lakes that can be reached only by packing in. Boats are usually unavailable. These shore-walking anglers take trout from seldom-fished waters. Golden trout are usually taken in this manner.

The more experienced anglers, however, usually don chest waders. I like the additional mobility chest waders give me in a lake. It is amazing how much water you can cover by wading most lakes. This is not true, of course, in the deep reservoirs with steep shorelines.

Usually, I'm reasonably comfortable in water up to my waist. But when the water begins to lap toward my wader tops, I'm inclined to seek shallower water.

Regardless of where you're wading, you should move cautiously. Slow, deliberate movement is less risky than haste and less likely to disturb the fish. When I wade, I like to slide my feet along, making sure my leading foot is planted solidly before I move the other. This is a good way to avoid sudden dropoffs or holes.

Though I'm more limited in my mobility when I'm wading than I am when I'm in a boat, I sometimes think I do a better job of fishing when I wade. Because I'm not moving far or rapidly, I tend to cover the water more thoroughly.

Chest waders are not absolutely essential for wading the shallows of a lake. But the better trout waters are cold, and you risk cramps or worse if you wade wet.

Fishing Methods Used on Lakes

Many anglers don't like to troll, and I must admit that I share their feelings to a degree. Still, trolling is a highly effective way to take trout in a lake. I believe many anglers relate trolling to the methods used for taking big lake trout from the depths on wire or lead-core lines and heavy weights. Even a big laker taken in this manner doesn't get a chance to display its true fighting abilities. Sometimes, unfortunately, it is the only way to catch lakers.

But what about trolling for the other trouts—brookies, browns, and rainbows, for example? Untold numbers of trout are taken by trolling, and many of them are of lunker size. It is usually the best way to fish a strange lake.

The electric trolling motor mentioned earlier can be used in slow trolling. But most anglers simply throttle down their gasoline outboards and have no trouble maintaining the proper trolling speed.

When the customary two anglers are in a boat, they should fish from opposite sides of the boat so as to avoid tangled lines. They should also be careful when making sharp turns. When one angler gets a fish, the other should reel in line to avoid a tangle and possibly a lost fish.

Moderate-to-heavy spinning tackle is fine for trolling, but the lures tend to twist the line, thereby creating bird nests on the reel. The twist can be removed periodically by taking off the lure and letting the bare line run out behind the fast-moving boat.

Some anglers use trolling as a means of locating trout. Once they catch a fish, they anchor and cast or fish natural baits.

For others, trolling is a basic angling method. Even those who continue to troll after taking that first fish make it a practice to swing their boats around to run back over the water that produced the trout—and they may continue to do so as long as it gives up fish.

Expert trollers do not fish blindly. Their success depends upon the water temperature, the season, and their ability to recognize the likely location of the trout.

Your trolling success also depends much upon your ability to vary the depth of your lure. You can do so in a number of ways. Varying the speed of the boat will change the depth of the lure, but this approach may not be desirable: it also changes the *speed* of the lure.

Sinkers are probably the most common means to vary trolling depth, but the type of lure is also a factor. Some lures run deep, others shallow. Again, the speed of the boat is a factor, for a lure with a long lip will dig deeply into the water when the speed of the boat is increased. You can also control the depth of your lure by varying the amount of line you have out.

During the early spring, often just after ice-out, trout feed heavily on the surface. It's a good time to take them by trolling, but the lure must be fished near the surface.

As the season progresses and the surface water warms, the trout will go deeper, seeking temperatures in the range of 55° to 65° F. The depth can be determined by lowering a thermometer that you can read at the surface. Spoons and spinners trolled at the depth with the preferred temperature will usually take trout.

Trolling can be good near shore when strong winds break up the surface and drive the temperature down. Baitfish will be near shore, and trolling parallel to shore can be good. Troll just fast enough to keep the lure barely beneath the surface.

As in all forms of angling, you should not hesitate to experiment when you're trolling. My largest rainbow trout to date was taken on a small streamer trolled in tiny Douthat Lake in Virginia. The season was early April, and I was headed for the dock. But as is my usual custom, I decided to troll as I rowed in. Many anglers pass up this opportunity.

I flipped the lure over the side and let out about twenty feet of line. I hadn't made a dozen strokes with the oars when the wildly vibrating rod told me I had a strike. Armed with ultralight spinning tackle entirely appropriate for the ten- to twelve-inch rainbows in the lake, I had a real tussle on my hands. Fortunately, I was able to get the big trout out into the middle of the lake, where I wore it down in the open water.

Several years ago my wife, daughter, and I flew by bush plane to a crystal-clear lake a hundred miles beyond the end of the road in northern Saskatchewan. We were there for big lake trout. The time was mid-June, but we flew through flurries of snow as the little plane drummed north.

We were on the lake fishing within fifteen minutes of landing. Within the next five minutes, I was fast to a small laker that fought like fury. The ice had been out of that northern lake just a couple of weeks, and the lakers were near the surface. I doubt that they had seen another angler that spring. We took most of them trolling just beneath the surface, but we also took a number of good ones by casting with spinning tackle.

Later that evening, our Indian guide filleted a couple of those orange-fleshed trout and broiled them over an open fire. We enjoyed the kind of feast you dream about.

A medium-action spinning rod and ten- to fifteen-pound-test line is adequate in trolling for lakers during the spring if the fish are in the shallows. In fact, during a recent spring, I took a fine ten-pounder from a Quebec lake on spinning tackle with eight-pound-test line.

By trolling straight out behind your boat you can take trout of all kinds in lakes. But many experienced trollers like to run lazy-S patterns with the boat. Such a strategy covers more water and causes the lure to change directions frequently—a tactic that will take trout.

Varying the speed of the boat is another popular trolling tactic. Trout often hit just as the lure begins to sink when the boat's speed is reduced.

A rule of thumb followed by experienced trolling anglers is to run the lure deep on bright days and shallow on cloudy, overcast ones.

Anglers who fish Utah's Flaming Gorge Reservoir, the home of the record brown trout, prefer the open water in May and June. They troll shallow with spinners, spoons, and small underwater plugs. Later, in the heat of July and August, they troll more slowly and much deeper—approximately fifteen to thirty feet.

A white bucktail trolled around points and over submerged reefs will take big browns in the lakes. The lure should be trolled just beneath the surface and manipulated with the rod tip so that it darts forward and occasionally swims off course. Browns can also be caught by trolling or by casting from a boat to the shore with plugs, spinners, and spoons. Generally, it is best to troll deep during the day, but in four to eight feet of water early in the morning and during late afternoon.

Trolling is usually best along the shore toward which the wind is blowing and piling up food.

Trolling does take trout of all kinds in lakes across the country, but there are many other effective methods.

One successful guide I know likes to jig for trout, particularly during the summer. He prefers a medium-weight spinning outfit, and for lures he uses jigs and spoons. He lowers his lure to the bottom in 60 to 100 feet of water, then reels it slowly back to the surface, constantly lowering and raising the tip of his rod. He expects most strikes to come when his lure is approximately halfway between the bottom and the lake's surface. Such a method requires good knowledge of the water and some idea where the trout will be at various times of the year. A fish finder is helpful.

Some anglers turn to jigging when their arms become weary of casting. Jigging's a good way to fish deep water during hot weather. Flip open the bail of your spinning reel and let the lure—usually a spoon—drop all the way to the bottom of the lake. When you feel it bump bottom, lift it a foot or two and then begin jigging it up and down.

A jig sweetened with a strip of fish such as the cisco makes a good lake-trout lure. Let the combination sink to the bottom, and retrieve it in short spurts.

Lake-trout anglers watch for swallows in the spring. When they see the birds diving on the surface of the water, they know the flies are hatching and attracting alewives or sawbellies. These baitfish in turn bring up the lakers. It is a good time to attach a nymph (without a hook) on a short dropper in front of a spoon. Cast this rig amidst the diving swallows, let it sink to the bottom, and retrieve it in short spurts. The spoon should be permitted to flutter to the bottom between spurts.

Worms, salmon eggs, and other natural baits cast from the shore of a lake will often take big trout. But to be successful this way you must make long casts—out where the trout are cruising. A heavy weight may be needed to get the distance, but if the trout feels the tug of the lead it may spit out the bait. One way to avoid this hazard is to copy the surf fisherman and use a sliding sinker, through which the line will run freely.

Some anglers use sugar cubes for weight, attaching a pair of them to the line with rubber bands a foot above the hook. The cubes provide sufficent casting weight and then slowly dissolve, giving you a free line out there among the big trout.

Even rainbows seem more willing to hit a dead bait in lakes and ponds than they are in streams. Rainbows can be taken on the bottom with worms, but many anglers like to keep the worm moving, hopping it slowly back to shore. The lake-dwelling rainbow is more inclined to hit a slow-moving bait than is its stream counterpart.

Because there is little or no current in lakes and ponds, the trout tend to cruise more than they do in streams. They often circle the smaller lakes, but in large lakes trout may limit their movement to the more productive water. Lake fishermen soon learn to take advantage of this tendency.

It may be best to remain in a spot the trout are accustomed to cruising, and let the trout come to you instead of your hunting for

A trout angler makes himself comfortable while using spinning tackle to fish for trout in Eagle Lake, called the best trout lake in New Mexico.

them. Such waiting is against the nature of many anglers, however.

When the water is clear and calm, you can often easily spot the cruising trout, especially if they are just below the surface or even deep in clear water. Casting just ahead of them can be a real challenge, but it can also be productive. It is a delicate situation in which you must maintain a low profile and limit yourself to side-casts so as not to spook the trout.

New Mexico anglers like to fish with scuds, casting them ahead of cruising trout in the clear mountain lakes. Then you retrieve in a stop-start action. The fishing is usually best at dusk when you can see the trout creating wakes as they chase the scuds. Early morning and late afternoon are generally the best times to fish for cruising trout; the water is more likely to be calm then.

Of course, you can wade the lake shallows and hunt for trout just as you do in streams, casting a variety of lures to dropoffs, stream mouths, rocks, weed beds, and other cover. One good way to fish an area thoroughly is to start casting facing in one direction parallel to shore and, with consecutive casts about a yard apart, cast until you have made a semicircle back to the shore and you're facing in the opposite direction.

As a lake angler hunting for trout, you can expect to cast a great variety of lures and at various depths until you locate the fish. You also vary the action of your lure—working it slowly, then fast, erratically, then letting it flutter and sink in crippled-minnow fashion.

In the high-country lakes of trout-rich Montana, big rainbows hit well for a couple of weeks after the melting of the ice. The trout may be fairly deep but close to shore off the rocky points on the side of the lake toward which the wind is blowing. It is a good time to fish for them with spoons, spinners, and small plugs cast from shore or even trolled behind a boat. Usually, the trout are reasonably well grouped at choice feeding stations.

Late one June day, I watched Steve Martinez—a conservation officer on the Jicarilla Apache Indian Reservation in New Mexico— take a fine creel of rainbows from a reservation lake by using a plastic bobber and dry flies.

"It's my favorite way to fish these lakes late in the day," he told me.

Wet flies can sometimes be fished just as effectively beneath a bobber.

Other high-country anglers like to fish natural baits with a bobber so they can control the depth at which the bait is suspended. The trout will usually hit best when the bait is being moved slowly, but they will hit a still bait as well.

High-altitude lakes like those found in California's High Sierra can be tough to fish. Successful anglers keep trying a variety of lures and methods until they hit a winning combination. They also like to fish areas in which several lakes are within walking distance. If one lake fails, they can try others.

A rainy day can be a good time for fishing clear lakes. The raindrops break up the surface and make you less conspicuous. A light breeze that ripples the water can have a like effect.

If you're seeking trout in a lake, you must above all be persistent. Other things being equal, the angler with an offering in the water the longest will catch the most trout.

Lures and Baits

As a lake angler, you ought to use in the relatively still areas lures of the same general types you'd use in streams, but generally they'll run larger. Lures that sink readily are an advantage in lake fishing because they need to penetrate deeper water. Lake-fishing lures generally have more built-in action because there is no current to provide a natural drift and produce the action needed to attract a trout's attention.

Natural baits (live minnows, particularly) seem to get more use in lakes than they do in the rivers.

The spoon is a favorite of anglers working the lakes, because it flutters or wobbles with the slightest movement, casts well, and sinks rapidly. Spoons probably take more trout from lakes than any other type of lure.

When you fish a lake, you'll usually reach for a spoon heavier than those the average stream angler is accustomed to. Trout run larger in lakes, and the bigger spoon is appropriate.

Since a large spoon hits the water with a good splash, your best tactic is to cast beyond the spot you expect the trout to be and then work it back to the fish. The spoon should be permitted to sink five to twenty seconds, depending upon how deep you want to fish. Count the seconds as the spoon sinks, and keep trying different depths until you get a strike. Then fix firmly in mind the count on which the strike came.

"Lake trout [the species] come into the shallows after smelt once the ice melts," Mal Taggar told me as we trolled the shoals of Big Cedar Lake in western Quebec one bright day in May. It's a good time to bump the gravel and rocks of the shoals with a big spoon. Silver or crystal finishes are good.

Spoons get heavy and widespread use: for brook trout in the high western lakes, for big browns in the Quabbin Reservoir in Massachusetts, for big lakers in Great Bear Lake in Canada's Northwest Territories. Many Great Bear Lake anglers fish light spinning tackle with eight-pound-test line.

Weighted streamers and wet flies take a lot of trout in the lakes, and these lures can be fished effectively on spinning tackle. Good patterns include the Barnes Special, Dark Tiger, Gray Ghost, Professor, Pumpkinseed, and Silver Minnow. Some reservoir anglers like to troll tandem or two-hook streamers such as the Grizzly King, Nine-Three, Pink Ghost, Spencer Bay, and Supervisor.

Streamers and flies can be fished with or without spinners. Much depends upon the condition of the water. Spinners are good in colored water, but they may be too flashy in extremely clear water.

Jigs or doll flies are probably best fished by jigging. But they cast well and sink rapidly, qualities that make them handy in deep water. They have no built-in action, so they're best retrieved in short jerks.

And, of course, there are the usual spinners and spinner–fly combination lures such as Mepps, Roostertail, and Panther/Martin. They are a good choice when you're in doubt. Anglers for golden trout like to work small spinners along the bottom in the high-altitude lakes in the west.

Plugs such as the Rapala, Rebel, and others get more use in lakes than they do in streams—mostly because of their appeal to bigger trout. Plugs that resemble baitfish are usually best in lakes. Most popular of the natural baits for lake fishing are minnows and baitfish of various kinds. Night crawlers and other worms also get heavy use. Live minnows fished deep in the lakes should be lowered gently so that they can adjust to the pressure. Otherwise they may die quickly.

Minnows are a good choice for late fall and winter fishing, when big rainbow trout feed on baitfish just before the cold of winter sets in. Minnows fished in lakes are best hooked by running the hook through the back just behind the dorsal fin and are usually dropped straight down in the water.

Live smelt, chubs, minnows, and other baitfish can be trolled successfully over lake shoals and bars and near inlets.

Worms are probably fished from the shore most of the time, either on the bottom or suspended beneath a bobber. My preference, however, is to cast them out from shore, let them settle to the bottom, and then retrieve them slowly in short hops.

Just about every insect imaginable is a possible bait for catching trout in the lakes, and the only limitation is their availability and your understanding of your quarry. Freshwater shrimp, hellgrammites, snails, nymphs, frogs—the list goes on—will all take trout under the right conditions. Generally, it is best to keep these baits moving slowly and in short jerks or twitches.

No other kind of water requires more experimenting than a big lake. But if you solve the puzzle, you'll be rewarded with some of the biggest trout in North America.

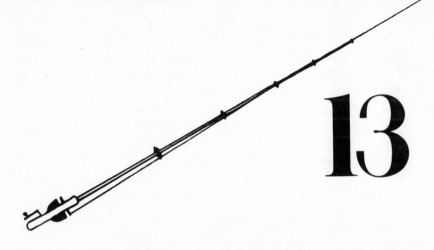

Spinning for Rainbows

The world has more than 100 subspecies of trout. But you needn't concern yourself with most of them.

Trout exist on every continent except Antarctica. Siberia has the greatest amount of trout habitat, and the largest trout in the world is the huchen found primarily in the Danube River of Europe, in Siberia, and in northern Japan. It may weigh more than 100 pounds.

The smallest trout in the world is a tiny char in Lake Constance on the Swiss–Austrian border. Its maximum length is six inches. The rarest trout in the world is the flatheaded trout of Turkey, and the rarest in the United States is the silver trout of Monadnock Lake in New Hampshire. In fact, it may be extinct.

The trout fisherman's possibilities are almost unlimited. Several dozen species of trout live within the United States and Canada. The family is large, and its members live in some of the wildest and most scenic country on this continent. Trout of one kind or another can be found from the frozen Arctic south to northern Georgia and the arid Southwest, and from coast to coast. Sea-run trout enter the briny waters of both the Atlantic and Pacific.

Fishery biologists have the various trouts well classified, though there is some doubt about where some of them originated. Occasionally, there is disagreement over classifications. For example, is the cutthroat really just another rainbow?

I like to consider the trouts in four groups—the rainbow, brook, brown, and cutthroat. It's an arrangement that serves anglers well, and it's the one I've been using in this book.

The only two native trout in the true sense are the rainbow and cutthroat, both western fish originally. There has even been some speculation that the original cutthroat was a cross between the rainbow and a char.

The brown trout is a native of Europe, successfully introduced to this continent before the turn of the century.

The brook trout is actually the best-known member of the char family, a group that includes the arctic char and the lake trout.

The rainbow is the trout most anglers know best. Closely related is the steelhead (a stream-reared rainbow that goes to sea), the Kamloops trout, the golden trout of the west, and a golden trout developed in recent years by West Virginia biologists.

The original range of the rainbow was from the Rocky Mountains to northern California and then north through western Canada to Alaska. There were also a few rainbows scattered through the upper Midwest.

Of all the trouts, the rainbow has responded best to fishery-management techniques, and it can be raised successfully and at reasonable expense in hatcheries. Today you can find excellent rainbow-trout fishing throughout most of Canada, Alaska, and the northern half of the United States. And the cool waters of the Appalachian and Rocky Mountain ranges permit the introduction of rainbows into states far south.

If the water is cool and clean, the rainbow can live in it. It prefers temperatures in the range of 50° F. to the low 60s, though the rainbow may feed in water of 70° F. and survive a while when the water temperature hits 80°.

Rainbow trout are taken from lakes as well as from streams. This four-pound, ten-ounce lunker was caught in Fontana Lake in western North Carolina by Jerry Estes. Photo by Michael Stewart

Good rainbow-trout waters are legion. Stocked trout survive to reproduce in tiny headwaters streams of the Appalachian Mountains and flourish in the icy tailwaters of the big impoundments in the southern half of the United States.

Mountain streams from Georgia, North Carolina, and Tennessee north offer rainbow-trout fishing, though much of it is the put-and-take variety: hatchery-reared fish. Many of these streams carry fish over from year to year, however, and then there is little difference between a hatchery fish and a wild one.

Fine fishing can be found in both lakes and streams throughout Canada, the northeastern United States, in the tributary streams of the Great Lakes, and in the tailwaters of dams on the White and Little Red rivers in the Ozarks.

In the rainbow's native west, such waters as Idaho's Snake River and its tributaries are good. But you're likely to find good rainbow-trout fishing just about anywhere in the west. On an antelope hunt in Wyoming one October, I found some excellent fishing in Clear Creek—a small stream draining the Big Horn Mountains and flowing through the city of Buffalo. There was good fishing within easy walking distance of a main highway.

The rainbow is noted for its thrilling leaps. It is a vigorous fish and full of fight.

The rainbow is colorful. A pink stripe runs the length of its flanks and is very pronounced against a cobalt-and-silver background. This coloring gives the fish its name. There are, however, many color variations, depending upon the water the rainbow lives in. Stream fish are heavily sprinkled with black spots, but lake fish may be almost pure silver. Some have bluish, gold, or bronze overtones. Its dark tail fin is marked with black spots. It lacks the cutthroat's red slash beneath its jaw, but during spawning time the male rainbow turns a bright red.

The rainbow has a soft anal fin of from ten to fourteen rays and a zigzag row of teeth on the roof of its mouth. It is a scaly fish with usually fewer than 150 scales in a row lengthwise of its body.

The average hatchery trout will measure ten to twelve inches, and such fish make up the catch of most anglers. Under ideal conditions, rainbows grow much larger. Fish of two to five pounds are not uncommon in good rainbow-trout country.

A happy Virginia angler shows off a big rainbow trout taken on spincasting tackle, a variation of spinning tackle. The lucky angler was fishing with live minnows. Photo by L. G. Kesteloo

Spring and fall are the prime fishing months, and dawn and dusk the most productive hours. But rainbows are taken throughout the year and at all hours of the day.

The spinning angler will find spoons, spinner–fly combinations, jigs, and weighted flies and streamers effective, but keep the lures small. A three-eighth-ounce lure is about the maximum. The retrieve should be reasonably fast, but it pays to experiment. Natural baits such as worms, minnows, crayfish, salmon eggs, and hellgrammites can be fished effectively on spinning tackle, but the bait should be kept moving. Kernels of corn and bits of cheese will also take rainbows.

Rainbows spend much of their time in the riffles, rapids, and other fast water, holding beneath it or to either side. Food moves rapidly in such water, and the rainbow lurking in the dead water behind a boulder or just outside the current is attuned to hitting hard and fast. This situation makes for exciting fishing.

Though usually considered separately, the steelhead of the western slope of the Rockies is a sea-run rainbow trout. It too is a native of the west. Because it has access to the Pacific Ocean, it usually enters the salt water early and spends much of its life there. Most steelheads return to the streams to spawn after two years in the ocean, and their arrival creates true angling fervor.

The Great Lakes and feeder streams such as the Au Sable, Big and Little Manistee, and Muskegon offer a similar type of fishing, though their rainbows are not steelheads in the same sense.

The time of steelhead spawning runs is erratic, occurring from February into November and varying from river to river. The peak of the run may even come in the summer in some streams.

The steelhead, though built along the same lines as the rainbow, is more silvery, and its back is usually varying shades of blue or green. The steelhead is a giant when compared to the rainbow. Fish of eight pounds are common, and even fifteen-pounders are not unusual in the better streams.

The strike of the steelhead—often just a tap—is much less dramatic than that of the rainbow. Most anglers ignore the extremes of water: the dead water, and water too fast to wade. The slicks, the tails or pools, and the swirling water at the top of a pool are good.

Most trout would avoid this fast, white water, but not the rainbow. This fish is a roamer and challenges all kinds of water.

Experienced anglers learn steelhead migration patterns and keep up with their movements.

Many steelheads are taken on spinning tackle, and they fall to a variety of lures—spoons, spinners, sacks of salmon eggs, and weighted flies and streamers such as the Comet, Muddler, Steelhead Bee, and Stone Nymph.

Another rainbow is the big Kamloops, a native of British Columbia but successfully introduced to the northwest United States. It feeds primarily on Kokanee salmon and grows to giant sizes. Fish of thirty pounds are fairly common. The Kamloops has all the markings of the typical rainbow but may be darkly or lightly hued depending upon the water it lives in.

Because the Kamloops feeds primarily on small salmon, streamers are a favorite lure, but where it's legal, most fish are probably taken on live kokanees fished deep. Spoons and wobblers are also good.

Biologists believe the little golden trout of the west may have descended from a strain of the rainbow, or from a rainbow-cut-throat hybrid. The golden interbreeds with the rainbow. It is found in the high country of California, Colorado, Idaho, Montana, Washington, and Wyoming.

Because the average golden lives in cold, infertile water, it's small. A three-pounder is a real lunker. The typical golden is olive along the back with crimson-marked gill covers and a swath of crimson along its flanks. The rest of the fish is yellow or orange. It is built along the lines of the rainbow.

Most goldens are taken on ultralight spinning tackle during July and August. Small lures such as spinners, spoons, flies, and streamers will take them—when they're hitting. Good natural baits include salmon eggs, grubs, and midges.

In the 1960s, West Virginia biologists developed their own golden trout, actually a rainbow mutation. These fish are stocked regularly in the state's put-and-take waters and offer a chance for an unusual catch.

Good rainbow-trout fishing of one kind or another is within the reach of most spinning anglers.

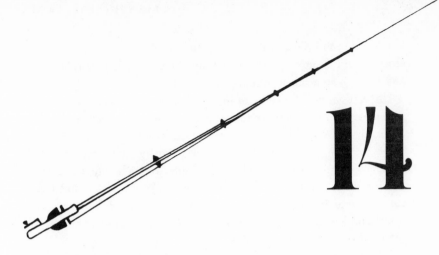

Brooks and Browns and All the Rest

Once you've sampled the joys of trout fishing on some sparkling rainbow waters, you may decide to try for other species.

If you're an easterner, chances are good your next trout will be a brookie—or possibly a hatchery-reared brown.

If you're a westerner, you may start with rainbows, but then the native cutthroat could well be your next trout.

Brook Trout

The colorful little brook trout, fondly known as the brookie, is the darling of eastern trout fishermen. Actually a char, it is native to the eastern United States and found as far south as the tip of the Blue Ridge Mountains in northern Georgia. It is also native across Canada from Labrador west to Saskatchewan.

Like the rainbow and the brown, the brook trout has been widely stocked and is now found throughout the west, where it reproduces naturally in some clear mountain streams.

Unfortunately, the colorful brookie never adapted to civilization. The clearing of forests, sedimentation of streams, and general deterioration of cool, clean waters drove the brook trout from much of its original range. Today, native brook trout live only in headwaters streams, remote from civilization, high in such rugged eastern mountains as the Blue Ridge, Alleghenies, Adirondacks, and Great Smokies and in the backcountry of Maine, New Hampshire, Vermont, and Michigan's Upper Peninsula. Canadian anglers also enjoy good fishing for native brookies.

The brook trout you find today are more likely to be hatchery-reared specimens, fish grown to catchable size in federal or state hatcheries and released in suitable put-and-take waters.

The native brook trout is a handsome fish. Its square tail is a distinct feature, and in many parts of its range the brookie is called squaretail. It is dark on the back with vermicular (wormlike) markings. Bright red spots encircled by light blue rings dot its typical orange or yellow flanks. The belly of the native fish is usually bright orange. Its lower fins are also typically orange and edged in white.

The brookie's scales are so tiny and insignificant that anglers rarely bother to scale their catch. Its fins are soft, and its tongue has no teeth.

Hatchery brookies are normally much paler.

Though fairly easy to catch, the brookie is extremely wary. Your shadow cast on a pool will send it scurrying for cover.

The traditional image of the brook trout is one of a leaping fish poised momentarily above a sparkling pool, its colorful flanks glistening. Actually, the brookie is not inclined to jump. It will take dry flies readily, but it is inclined to wage its battle beneath the surface.

In the tiny streams where most anglers know it best, the brookie is a small fish. A twelve-incher is a lunker. The average creel is more likely to be made up of eight- and nine-inchers. In lakes and ponds, however, the fish run larger, and so do the sea-run brookies—nicknamed "salters"—along the coast of Labrador and in other eastern streams that enter the ocean. Fish of two to four pounds are fairly common in such waters.

*This big lake trout was taken on spinning tackle by Donald Sau-
muke out of Big Cedar Lake in western Quebec. Saumuke guides
anglers out of Moosehead Lodge on the lake.*

In streams, brook trout tend to congregate in the quiet water, the pools and backwaters off the main current. A brookie ventures into the riffles and rapids during early morning and evening feeding periods. It seems to thrive best in cold, clean water, over soft, mud-covered bottoms, and in beaver ponds on small streams.

Brook trout will hit a great variety of both natural and artificial baits, but few are more effective than ordinary garden worms fished on ultralight spinning tackle. The angler after big brookies should try Mepps and Colorado spinners and Daredevle spoons in large sizes, and work them slowly.

The native brook trout is a fish for all seasons. Where it's legal, ice fishermen sometimes take them during the dead of winter.

The brook trout, the most popular of the chars, has many relatives.

The big lake trout is perhaps the most popular. It is a northern fish found from northern New York and New England west to the Great Lakes and north to Alaska, and in the deep lakes of the northwest and Canada.

The lake trout's popularity has suffered because most specimens are taken by trolling deep in the big lakes with heavy tackle. Not much fun. But lakers taken soon after ice-out in the shallows and on medium-weight spinning tackle are a different story.

The laker goes by a variety of names—togue, Great Lake trout, mackinaw, forktail trout, salmon trout, and others. The typical lake trout is gray with pale spots all over its body, head, and tail. It grows big. The average laker runs eight to ten pounds, and twenty-pounders are reasonably common.

On the table, the laker is—in my opinion—the tastiest of all the trouts.

Most of the other chars are extremely limited in range. Among them are the Sunapee trout of New Hampshire; the Dolly Varden of the far west, Canada, and Alaska; the arctic char found across northern Canada and in Alaska; the Quebec trout of the Laurentians in Quebec; the blueback trout of Maine (but extremely rare); the aurora trout of northeastern Ontario; and the splake—a hardy char that is a cross between the brook trout and lake trout. It has been stocked in Canada and the northern United States.

Brown trout, introduced to America from Europe, have become very popular and widely stocked. This lunker brown was taken from Strawberry Lake in northern Utah. Photo by Utah Travel Council

Brown Trout

The brown trout, the idol of the dry-fly fisherman, is also worth the attention of the spinning angler. Like the rainbow, the brown is a true trout, not a char.

Though now very much at home in American waters, the brown is not a native fish. The ancestors of our browns came from European waters—some from Germany, some from England, some from Scotland and others from elsewhere in Europe.

Best known as the brown, the fish is often referred to as the European brown, German brown, and Loch Leven.

Because it will tolerate marginal waters better than will the brook and rainbow, the brown is found often where other trout won't survive. There are often good self-sustaining populations in the better waters. Generally, the brown is found from northern Georgia and California north.

Along the coast of New England, browns sometimes enter the Atlantic coastal waters and are known as salters. They return to the streams, silvery, strong, and full of vim. A like situation occurs in the Great Lakes region where the browns enter the big lakes from feeder streams. These fish return to the rivers for spawning, usually in late summer or fall.

The brown is the wariest of the trouts, and its shyness can exasperate anglers.

The brown's back is usually dark brown, but this shade varies according to the water it lives in. Its sides and belly fade to a lighter brown, bronze, or yellow. Its flanks are littered with black or blue spots and usually a few big red ones. The adult brown's tail is square, about like the brookie's.

The average brown will weigh less than a pound, but some specimens grow big. A U.S. record came from Utah's Flaming Gorge Reservoir in 1977—a big thirty-three-pound, ten-ounce brown trout.

The famous Beaverkill in New York's Catskill Mountains is one of the best brown-trout waters I've been privileged to fish. But good ones are numerous—the Letort in Pennsylvania; the Brule in Wisconsin; the Manistee in Michigan; and the Big Hole, Yellowstone, Gallatin, Madison, and Missouri in Montana.

Brown trout prefer the quieter, deep holes of the rivers and will tolerate warmer water than most other trout.

The brown likes the quieter water and seems to prefer the deep holes near the stream banks. It will also frequent the meandering stretches of meadow streams and the slicks of the fast water.

Stubborn and strong, the brown has a fighting heart, but it seldom leaps as does the rainbow. The brown knows how to take care of itself. Cagey and wary, it can survive in heavily fished waters. It knows the ways of anglers, and small browns often grow to adulthood in heavily fished waters while brookies and rainbows are filling anglers' creels.

Because the brown trout is predominantly an insect eater, it's a favorite of dry-fly fishermen, but the brown will also take bait and spinning lures. Spinning accounts for some of the larger fish. Spoons, wobblers, plugs, or other spinning lures will take browns.

The brown trout is nearly the equal of the lake trout and cutthroat when it comes to feeding on minnows. Night crawlers on a size 6 hook are also good. Run the hook first through the head and then beneath the collar. Worms are particularly good in the high, roily waters in the spring. They should be fished in the deep runs, the foot of rapids, the channels, and the tops of pools. Bounce the worm along the bottom. The high, muddy water conceals you and tends to move the browns from their hiding places.

Unique in trout fishing is the preference of brown-trout anglers for night fishing. Some real lunkers are taken then, but night fishing for trout is illegal in some states. It's tricky fishing—particularly on the streams. Most casts are made across the stream or downstream. Good offerings include live minnows; bass lures; a wide variety of spinners, spoons, and wobblers; and big streamers. Bushy wet flies and bucktails are also good. Such lures are best fished on spinning tackle.

Cutthroat Trout

The cutthroat, like the rainbow, is a native of the west. Originally, it was found along both slopes of the Continental Divide, whereas the rainbow was found along only the western slope. But today the rainbow is more adaptable and more widespread. The cutthroat has been driven from much of its original range, as has the brookie in the east.

Westerners consider the cutthroat their native trout. Some authorities say it was the progenitor of the rainbow. Rainbows have been introduced to many prime cutthroat waters, and the result has been a good bit of hybridization. Usually, however, the rainbow becomes the dominant species.

The name *cutthroat* comes from the twin slashes of red on the underside of the fish's jaw. Familiarly known as the cut to many anglers, the cutthroat is also called the Rocky Mountain trout, black-spotted trout, Colorado River trout, mountain trout, or west-slope cutthroat.

The fish looks much like the rainbow trout but is thicker and more rounded. The forward part of its body appears heavier than the rear. The entire body and the anal fin are often heavily spotted. The cutthroat's mouth appears larger than that of the rainbow, and it has teeth at the base of its tongue. The pink longitudinal stripe, dark back, and light belly are much like the coloration of the rain-bow.

Though the cutthroat lacks the dash and leaping battle tactics of the rainbow, it's a tough and determined fighter, usually staying deep, but occasionally leaping in an apparent effort to throw a lure.

Cutthroats vary tremendously in size. Headwaters fish may run only six to ten inches, but Alaska trout will average twelve to twenty-four inches. The sea-run cutthroats along the Pacific coast will average two to four pounds, and cuts in the big lakes may run twenty to forty pounds.

Fishery biologists have recently perfected the hatchery rearing of cutthroats, and the fish are being stocked widely in the west.

Cutthroats are found from sea level to ten thousand feet and in waters ranging from big lakes and torrential rivers to tiny creeks and beaver ponds high in the Rockies. The range includes the Rocky Mountains from California to Alaska.

In habits and water preference, the cutthroat is closer to the brookie than to the rainbow. The cutthroat likes deep holes beneath the banks of streams, logjams, and in general the quieter water. It generally avoids the rapids, riffles, and fast water favored by the rainbow.

The cutthroat has a weakness for a flashing spoon, a handy bit of information for a spinning angler. It is a willing striker and a joy to fish for. Cuts will also take spinners and wobblers, but these lures should be fished deep and slow. Wet flies and nymphs are also good.

The common garden-variety worm is high on the list of natural baits for cuts. It too should be fished deep and slow. The cutthroat feeds more on baitfish than most trout do, so minnows are excellent cutthroat bait.

Among the best cutthroat waters in North America today are the Snake River, Yellowstone Lake and River, the Wind, Greene, and Shoshone rivers in Wyoming, the Yellowstone tributaries in Montana, and Pend Oreille and Priest lakes in Idaho.

There are a number of variations of the cutthroat, fish peculiar to a certain stream, lake, or region—fish distinctive in coloration.

Possibly better known than even the true cutthroat is the Yellow-stone trout. This gaudily marked trout of the famous Yellowstone Lake has been caught by untold numbers of tourist anglers. A popular spot is the Fishing Bridge, where the Yellowstone River leaves the lake.

The Piute trout is a long, slender cutthroat with fragile fins. Biologists say it is an isolated strain of the Lake Tahoe cutthroat, and it is found in only the small streams of Fish Valley on the east slope of the Sierra Divide.

The Gila trout and its close kin the Apache trout are cutthroat variants that live only in the southwest. The Apache lives primarily on the Fort Apache Indian Reservation, the Gila in the Gila River drainage system of Arizona and New Mexico.

Big Lake Tahoe and the waters of the Truckee River system are home to the Lake Tahoe cutthroat, a large and silvery trout taken often in deep water.

The Lake Crescent trout is a cutthroat found only in the state of Washington, and the Montana black-spotted trout is another cut with limited range.

Finally, there is the famed harvest trout, the sea-run cutthroats that gather off the mouths of the major streams toward the end of summer, just when crops are being harvested on the West Coast. The fish are hungry and forage fish are scarce in the lower stretches of the streams. The cuts hit willingly, often causing farmers to forsake their harvesting to get in on the action.

But harvest time can be just about anytime in the rich and varied trout waters of North America, and nobody is better prepared than the well-equipped spinning angler to reap a share of the harvest.

Index